Wire & Bead
Celtic
Jewelry

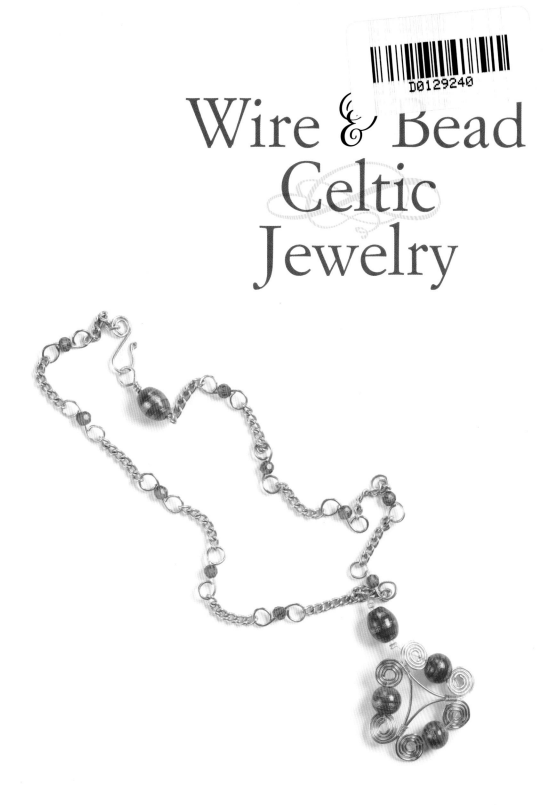

Wire & Bead Celtic Jewelry

35 quick & stylish projects

linda jones

CICO BOOKS

London   New York

DEDICATION

This book is dedicated to my loving partner, Chris, who allows me the freedom
to express myself through fiddling with wire and beads. Also, to my most
wonderful sons, Ben and Charlie, who uncomplainingly put up with the chaos
of a photo shoot in the house and finally, to my parents, Hans and Marian,
who are always there for me.

First published in 2007 by Cico Books
an imprint of Ryland, Peters & Small
519 Broadway 5th Floor
New York NY10012

10 9 8 7 6 5 4 3 2 1

Text & project designs copyright © Linda Jones 2007
Design & photography copyright © Cico Books 2007

A CIP catalog record for this book is available from the Library of Congress

ISBN-10: 1 904991 56 4
ISBN-13: 978 1 904991 56 4

Printed in China

Editor: Sarah Hoggett
Designer: David Fordham
Illustrator: Stephen Dew
Photographer: Caroline Arber
Stylist: Julie Hailey

contents

introduction

The Celts date back to about 500 BCE and were made up of many tribes, spread from Scotland and Ireland in the north-west, to Russia in the east, and down as far as the Mediterranean in the south. During the Roman period, many of the Celts were pushed into rough, less hospitable areas, but their culture continued to thrive and survived unchanged in Ireland, Scotland, Wales, and parts of France.

Celtic art has some of the finest examples of ornamentation ever created in stone, metalwork, and jewelry. The patterns are incredibly complex, with a knotwork of interlacing detail—limbs and bodies of humans, animals, birds, and reptiles as well as pure abstract decoration in key or geometric patterns, spirals, and swirls.

I often use colored wires to replicate the flowing lines and jewelike colors of ancient illuminated manuscripts in my Celtic-style jewelry.

Initially, I found designing the projects in this book quite a challenge, as my research came up with some stunning examples of chunky, bronze castings, scabbards, and chalices, but no traces of fine wirework at all! However, the more I studied linear detail on objects from ancient burial sites and the surviving pages of illuminated manuscripts, the more I realized that I could extract elements that could be simplified and reworked as wire-jewelry designs.

As wire is the main ingredient of each project in this book, I began by looking at Celtic metalwork. The metal most commonly used by the Celts was bronze (an alloy of copper and tin), which was worked either in sheet form, as inlay or embossed decoration, or as raised surface ornamentation, shaped over a mold with decoration engraved into the exterior. I have tried to reinterpret this solid metal rendering by twisting and braiding wires together, as in the Braided and Twisted Torque Bangles on pages 54 and 56. Color also played a significant part in enhancing Celtic metalwork, with coral in particular being inlayed onto shields and scabbards, as well as brooch pins. Other natural resources used were shells, amber, and semiprecious stones set in as embellishments, as well as red glass or "enamel," which was sunk into the original castings. I have used colored glass beads and semiprecious chip stones threaded on wire as the modern-day equivalent.

Stone carvings were another important source of motifs and inspiration for my jewelry designs. With the advent of Christianity, many Celtic patterns and motifs were incorporated into Christian Celtic art,

The spiral in Celtic art represents the never-ending cycle of life, and is a classic—and instantly recognizable—motif in Celtic ornamentation.

as can be seen in the remains of the stones and crosses. The triskele and the 3-C scroll motifs, in particular, in which a pattern of three curves radiates out at equal intervals from one central axis, symbolizing the Christian trinity or the cycle of life, can be found repeated in numerous pieces of stone work.

I also took much of my inspiration from the linear swirls and spirals found in the knotwork borders of illuminated manuscripts such as the Book of Kells and the *Lindisfarne Gospels* and used colored beads and wire to replicate the jewelike colors of natural pigments and stones. The use of a jig allowed me to duplicate the repeat patterns, as in the Lindisfarne Choker (page 80).

Finally, I considered the other natural materials and resources that the Celts would have had at their disposal, such as pebbles, shells, wood, bone, and leather. The Wrapped Stone Pendant (page 90) and the Pebble and Shell Charm Bracelet

(page 50) require semiprecious "pebbles" and shells and could very well have existed as protective, talismanic jewelry for the wearer. The Butterfly Necklace (page 102), with its knotted cord, is reminiscent of knotwork borders, and the Valentine Knot Bracelet (page 48) and Kilt Pin (page 30) have wood- and bone-effect beads reflecting the natural ingredients of those times.

It is immensely difficult, if not impossible, to recreate the style of a bygone age, particularly one as rich and varied as that of the Celts. However, I have attempted to remain true to the spirit of the Celtic artisans, while using modern-day materials and techniques. I hope that you will not only enjoy creating and adapting my jewelry designs to suit your own style and color schemes, but that, like me, you will rediscover the incredible skill and craftsmanship of this ancient culture.

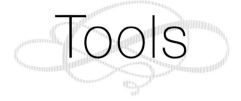

Tools

The tools shown on these two pages are virtually all you need to make wire and beaded jewelry and are readily available from craft suppliers, mail-order catalogs and, of course, the Internet. For more information on suppliers, turn to page 126.

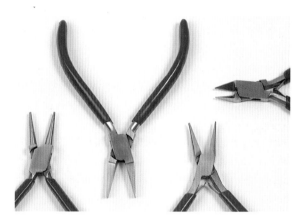

From left to right: Round-nose pliers, flat-nose pliers, chain-nose pliers, wire cutters.

Pliers and cutters

You will need a good pair of wire cutters and two or three kinds of pliers. There are three types of pliers used in making wire jewelry—round-nose, flat-nose, and chain-nose—although, to get started, round- and flat-nose are the most essential. It is well worth investing in good-quality versions.

ROUND-NOSE PLIERS have tapered shafts, around which you bend the wire—so they are ideal for coiling and bending wire into small loops or curves, as well as for creating jump rings.

FLAT-NOSE PLIERS have flat, parallel jaws. They are used to grip the wire firmly as you work with it, and to bend it at right angles, as well as to neaten and flatten ends so that no sharp wires stick out. They are smooth-jawed, with no serrations or grips, as this would mark the wire when held.

CHAIN-NOSE PLIERS are similar to flat-nose pliers, but have tapered ends. They are useful for holding very small pieces of wire and for fabricating more intricate and delicate pieces, as well as for bending angular shapes in wire.

WIRE CUTTERS are available in several forms, but I find that "side cutters" are the most useful, as they have small, tapered blades that can cut into small spaces. Always hold the cutters perpendicular to the wire when cutting to achieve a clean cut.

Jig

A jig is used to form elaborate loops and wire patterns. Jigs are readily available from craft stores. Alternatively, you can make your own from a block of wood and some carpenter's nails.

A jig consists of a base board with a series of evenly spaced holes and moveable pegs with tops of different diameters, which you arrange in a pattern of your choosing. You then wrap wire around the pegs to create a decorative wire design. The benefit of using a jig is that it enables you to replicate the design as many times as you wish, in the certainty that each unit will be identical.

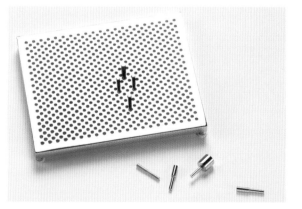

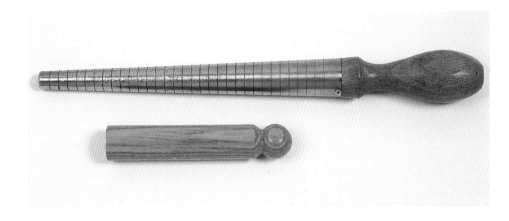

Right: A specialist ring mandrel (top), marked with gradations showing standard ring sizes, and an improvized mandrel (bottom)—a short length of wooden dowel.

Hammer and flat steel stake

These tools are used to flatten and toughen wire motifs (see page 21), so that they can take the strain of being worn without distorting and falling apart. You can use almost any kind of hammer, provided it has a smooth, flat steel end, although specialist jewelry hammers are generally small and lighter than general-purpose household hammers, so you may find them easier to use.

Steel stakes can be bought from specialist jewelry stores. As with hammer heads, the surface of the stake must be polished smooth, otherwise the wire will pick up any irregularities that are present. Always keep the hammer head at right angles to the wire being hit, otherwise you will obtain a textured surface.

Mandrel

To form circular shapes such as rings, bangles, and choker rings, you will need a mandrel. You can buy purpose-made mandrels in varying sizes. If you don't want to go to the expense of buying one, improvize by shaping your wire around any cylindrical object of the appropriate size. Wooden dowels from your local home-improvements store are an inexpensive option, but you could also use a glass jar or bottle, a rolling pin, or a curtain pole.

Hand drill and vise

These are not essential tools, but they are useful for twisting several lengths of wire together (see page 17). A small vise that you can attach to the edge of your work table is also a helpful tool to have if you are braiding wire (see page 17), as it holds one end of the wires firmly together while you work—although you could ask a friend to help.

Left: A jig and pegs with tops of different diameters. In some jigs, the holes are arranged in horizontal rows; in others, such as the one shown here, they are arranged on the diagonal.

Above: A jewelry hammer and steel stake, used to flatten and work-harden wire motifs.

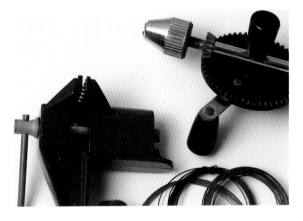

Above: A hand drill and vise— useful for twisting and braiding wires.

Materials

There is such a wonderful array of beautiful beads, colorful wires, and findings available that you will be spoilt for choice! If this is your first step into wire jewelry making, you'll enjoy bead browsing. In fact, the difficulty will be deciding when to stop!

Wire

Wire is available in many thicknesses, types, and colors. Colored, copper, and plated wires can be bought from most craft and hobby stores, as well as from bead suppliers. With the exception of precious metal, wire is generally sold in spools of a pre-measured length. Precious-metal wire is bought by length, the price being calculated by weight.

Colored wires are usually copper based, with enamel coatings, which means that they cannot be hammered or over-manipulated as this might

remove the surface color and look unsightly. Instead of precious-metal wires, I almost always use gold- or silver-plated wires, which are far less expensive. The only exception to this is if you need to file the wire, (as in the Beaded Bar Brooch on page 38), as filing the pin end will expose the copper core underneath the plating and look unattractive. Therefore, sterling-silver wire is essential for this particular design.

All these kinds of wire come in different thicknesses. Depending on where you buy your wire, different measurements are used to denote the thickness of the wire. The chart below will enable you to convert quickly from one system to another. The most commonly used general-purpose wire for jewelry making is 20-gauge (0.8 mm).

0.4 mm	28-gauge	Binding, knitting, and weaving
0.6 mm	24-gauge	Threading small delicate beads; binding and twisting
0.8 mm	20-gauge	General-purpose jewelry work
1.0 mm	18-gauge	Chunkier pieces and ring shanks
1.2 mm	16-gauge	Bolder, chunkier jewelry
1.5 mm	14-gauge	Very chunky, metallic wire jewelry

LEFT: Copper-, gold-, and silver-plated wires are less expensive than the precious-metal versions but look just as convincing.

RIGHT: Colored wires are available in a multitude of bright, modern colors.

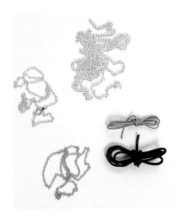

Left: Ready-made findings come in a variety of colors and finishes.

Right: Using ready-made chains and cords speeds up the process of making a necklace or bracelet—although you can, of course, make your own chains if you prefer.

Findings

Findings is the term used to describe ready-made components such as chains, ear wires and clips, barrettes and so on. They can be bought from craft and hobby stores. If you are using a ready-made chain in a design, check that the links are large enough to take whatever thickness of wire you use for the embellishments. If they are not large enough, make jump rings (see page 16).

Beads

Beads are made from all kinds of materials including glass, porcelain, plastic, metal, wood, and bone. Specialist bead stores contain thousands of different sizes and types, arranged by both color and size, and I defy anyone to visit such a store without buying something! Semiprecious chip stones and bone- or wood-effect beads are lovely beads to use on Celtic-style jewelry, as similar materials might well have been used by the Celts. Tiny seed beads—usually sold in tubes—are useful as "stopper" beads but, because they are so tiny, if you want them to have any impact in a design you generally need to string several together. Pre-drilled shells also make lovely beads—and you can even use objects without a pre-drilled hole, such as small pebbles, by wrapping wire around them, as in the Pebble and Shell Charm Bracelet on page 50.

When buying beads, always check that the wire you intend to use fits through the bead hole, as there is no correlation between the size of a bead and the diameter of its hole. If you can't find beads that exactly match the ones that I've used in the projects in this book, buy something of a similar size.

Found objects, such as pebbles and shells, could well have been used by the Celts as talismans or charms, and make striking "beads" for Celtic-style jewelry.

Try to think about the kinds of materials that the Celts would have had at their disposal. Wooden and bone-effect beads such as these are particularly appropriate.

Glass beads range from completely transparent to almost opaque. They can be expensive, so they are perhaps best used as "focal" beads for maximum impact.

basic techniques

If this is your first attempt at wire jewelry making, practice all the basic techniques to become totally familiar with the fundamentals of wire working and become acquainted with your tools, as well as to get a "feel" for your main ingredient—wire.

1. Following your chosen pattern, place the pegs in the jig. Using your round-nose pliers, form a loop at the end of your length of wire and slip it over the first peg.

2. Pull the wire around the pegs, following the pattern. You will need to keep pushing the wire down to the base of the pegs in order to keep the motif reasonably flat. Carefully remove the wire unit from the pegs.

Using a jig

As there are a number of different styles and types of jig on the market, you may find that you have to adjust the patterns in this book slightly. I suggest that, before you attempt any of the jig projects, you place your pegs as directed and then wrap a piece of cord or string approximately the same gauge as the wire that will be used around the pegs, following the pattern. Measure the amount of cord or string that you have used so that you know how much wire you will need to make the project, and then cut your wire to this length.

Once you have made your wire motif, you can reinforce it by gently tapping the outer edges of the wire with a hammer on a steel stake, being careful not to hammer any crossed-over wires, as this will weaken them (see page 21). Finally, spend a little time readjusting the wire with your flat-nose pliers and fingers until you are satisfied with the overall shape of your motif.

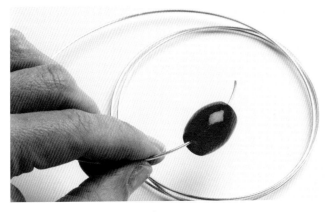

1. Working from the spool, thread your chosen bead onto the wire, leaving about ½ in. of wire extending on each side of the bead with which to form the link.

Threading beads with wire

The basic principle is to construct a neat loop of wire (known as a "link") at each end of the bead, which is then used to suspend the bead from a chain or to connect one bead to another.

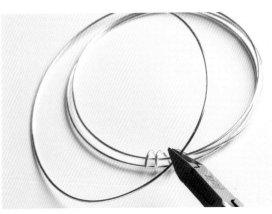

2. Remove the bead and cut the wire with your wire cutters.

3. Thread the bead back onto the cut wire. Holding the wire vertically, with the bead in the center, use the tips of your round-nose pliers to bend the wire at a right angle, at the point where it touches the bead.

When you've threaded the bead, make sure that the links at each end face in the same direction—otherwise they will twist around when linked together as a chain. To do this, hold each link firmly in the jaws of your pliers, and twist until both links face the same way.

4. Hold the very end of the bent wire tightly with your round-nose pliers, and curl it toward you into a circle. It is better to do this in several short movements, repositioning the pliers as necessary, than to attempt to make one continuous circle. Repeat Steps 3 and 4 to form another link at the other end of the bead. Remember, the pliers are not a levering tool but primarily a molding tool.

Making a head pin

If you want to suspend a bead from a chain, you will only need a suspension link at one end of the bead. At the other end, you need to make what is known as a "head pin," which is virtually invisible but prevents the bead from slipping off the wire.

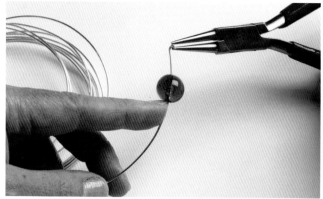

1. Working from the spool, thread your chosen bead onto the wire, leaving about ½ in. of wire extending on each side of the bead.

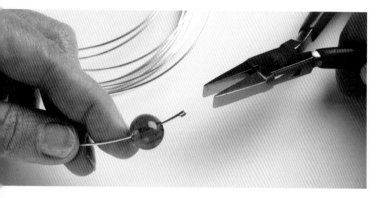

2. Using the tips of your round-nose pliers, make a tiny curl at one end of the wire. Squeeze this curl flat with your flat-nose pliers to create a small knob of wire.

3. Snip the wire and form a link at the other end. If the hole in the bead is large and it slips over the head pin, bend the head pin at a right angle, so that the bead sits on top of it like a tiny shelf. (Alternatively, slide on a small seed bead to act as a stopper.)

The head pin is unobtrusive, but it prevents the bead from slipping off the wire.

You can also make a decorative feature of the head pin by curling the wire into a spiral (see page 15). To do this, you will need to leave a longer length of wire below the bead.

Making spirals

The spiral is probably the most characteristic and distinctive symbol of Celtic style. There are two kinds of spiral—open and closed. Each is formed in the same way, the only difference being whether or not any space is left between the coils.

Both types of spiral begin by curling a circle at the end of the wire. The size of this circle depends on the design of your project. Sometimes, as in the Double Spiral Necklace on page 62, the circle needs to be as small as possible, so that there are virtually no gaps in the spiral. At other times, as in the Shamrock Hair Grip on page 116, you may want to feed a wire or cord through the spiral, so you need to make the initial circle bigger.

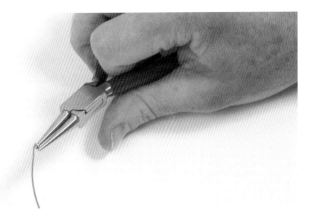

1. Begin by curling a small circle at the end of the wire, using the tips of your round-nose pliers. Make this circle as round as possible, as the rest of the spiral will be shaped around it.

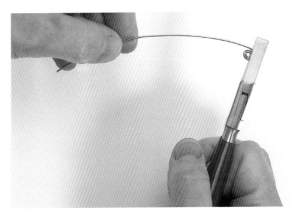

2. Grip the circle in your flat-nose pliers, and begin curling the wire around it. For a closed spiral, butt each coil up against the previous one. For an open spiral, leave space between the coils.

A closed spiral has no gaps between the coils. An open spiral is made in the same way, but evenly spaced gaps are left between the coils.

3. When the spiral is the size you want, leave about ½ in. of wire to form a suspension link, curling the projecting end of wire into a small loop in the opposite direction to the spiral.

Making jump rings

Jump rings are used to connect units together. You can buy them ready made, but it is well worth learning how to make them yourself as you can then match the jump rings to the color and size of wire that you are using. It is also much less expensive to make them yourself.

Jump rings are made by forming a wire coil around the shaft of your round-nose pliers, out of which you snip individual rings as required. When you bring the wire around the pliers to begin forming the second ring of the coil, it needs to go below the coil, nearer your hand. This keeps the wire on the same part of the pliers every time. If you bring the wire round above the first ring of the coil, the jump rings will taper, following the shape of the pliers' shaft.

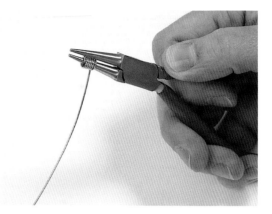

1. Working from the spool, wrap wire five or six times around one shaft of your round-nose pliers, curling it around the same part of the pliers every time to create an even coil.

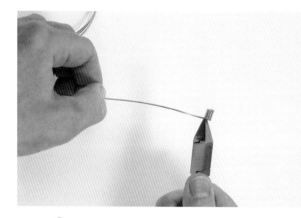

2. Remove the coil from the pliers and cut if off from the spool of wire using your wire cutters.

3. Find the cut end and, using your wire cutters, snip upward into the next ring of the coil, thereby cutting off a full circle. Continue cutting each ring off the coil in turn to obtain more jump rings.

Using jump rings to connect units

Using your flat-nose pliers, open one of the jump rings sidewise (like a door), so that you do not distort the shape. Loop the open jump ring through the links of the beads and close it with flat-nose pliers. The two ends of the jump rings should move just past one another, as the wire will spring back slightly when you remove the pliers. If you don't push the wires hard enough you will end up with a gap, which may mean that the beads will work loose.

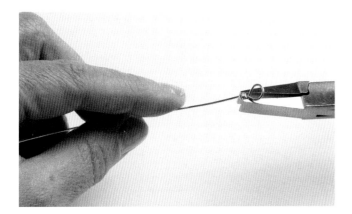

Neatening ends

When you've wrapped one piece of wire around another—as when making a clasp, for example—it's important to neaten the ends to prevent any sharp pieces from sticking out and snagging on clothing or scratching the wearer.

Snip the wire as close as possible to the stem with your wire cutters, and press it firmly with your flat-nose pliers to flatten it against the piece of jewelry.

Twisting wires together

Twisting wires together is not only fun and quick, but can provide a bolder, more metallic feel to your pieces. Celtic craftsmen would have cast a lot of their pieces in bronze, so to achieve a chunkier, more authentically Celtic-looking effect (as in the Twisted Torque Bangle on page 56), twist six to eight wires together.

I recommend using a vise and hand drill for this technique, as it is both quick and effective. If you do not have these tools, however, attach one end of your wires to a door handle or nail and the other to a wooden handle, such as a wooden spoon and, keeping the wires straight and taut, twist them in the same direction until you achieve the effect you want.

Always twist wires of the same thickness. If you end up with an uneven twist or bumps in your wire, it just means that some of the wires were longer or looser than others!

Braiding wires

You can braid wire in exactly the same way as hair or ribbon. Select your wires and bind them all together at one end with a small piece of masking tape. Secure in a vise and cross the left wire over the central one. Then cross the right wire over the central one and continue in this way until the braid is complete.

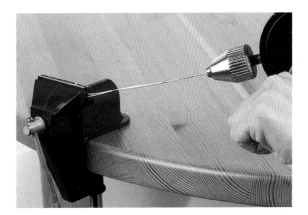

Bind the ends of the wires with masking tape. Place one end in the chuck of the hand drill and the other end in the vise. Hold the hand drill so that the wires are straight and taut, and gently turn the handle in one direction. (Do not twist too much or the wires will lose flexibility and become weak and brittle.) When the twist is complete, remove the wires from the hand drill and vise and snip off the taped ends.

Fish-hook clasp

The most commonly used clasp is the fish-hook, which is also one of the simplest to create.

1. Working from the spool, curl the end of the wire into a small loop using the tips of your round-nose pliers. Reposition your pliers on the other side of the wire, just under the loop, and curl the wire in the opposite direction around the wider part of the pliers to form the fish-hook clasp.

This hook-shaped clasp is both decorative and functional.

2. Cut the wire off the spool, leaving about ½ in. to form a link (see page 13). If you wish, you can gently hammer the hook on a steel stake to work-harden and flatten it slightly, thereby making it stronger and more durable.

Spiral clasp

Continue the Celtic theme of your jewelry by making a spiral-shaped clasp.

1. Make an open spiral (see page 15) of the appropriate size, then cut the wire off the spool leaving about ½ in. for the link.

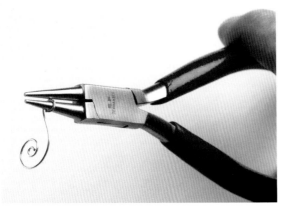

2. Using the tips of your round-nose pliers, form the end of the wire into a link (see page 13).

3. Gently hammer the spiral on a steel stake to flatten and work-harden it—but do not hammer the link.

S-shaped clasp

An S-shaped clasp is another popular decorative clasp with a Celtic feel.

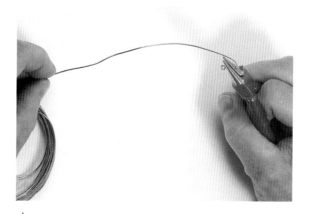

1. Working from the spool, curl a tiny loop at the end of the wire, using the tips of your round-nose pliers. Place the widest part of your pliers just under the loop and curve the wire in the opposite direction.

2. Cut the wire off the spool, turn the piece over and make a small loop at the other end of the wire.

3. Place the widest part of your pliers just under the loop, and curve the wire in the opposite direction to create a mirror image to the first curve and complete the "S" shape.

A basic S-shaped clasp, which has been gently hammered to flatten and toughen it.

Adding a bead before you form the second curve of the S-shape makes an attractive variation on the basic technique.

The "eye" of the fastener

This "eye" can be used to complete all the clasps used in this book—fish-hook, S-shaped, and spiral.

The completed eye, which can be linked to the ends of a necklace or bracelet either directly or via jump rings.

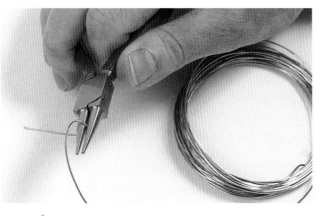

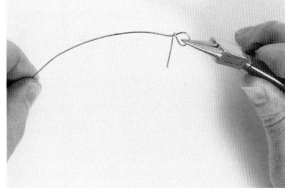

1. Working from the spool, curl a piece of wire around the widest part of your round-nose pliers about 1 in. from the end of the wire to form a loop, crossing the end of the wire over itself.

2. Wrap the extending wire around the stem, just under the loop.

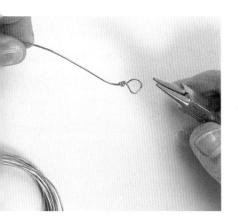

3. Cut the wire off the spool, leaving about ½ in. extending. Using the tips of your round-nose pliers, form the extending wire into a link (see page 13).

4. Gently hammer the "eye" on a steel stake to flatten and toughen it. Do not hammer the wires that have been wrapped over the stem or you will weaken them.

Coiled fish-hook clasp and fastener

This is a variation on the basic fish-hook clasp. It is used on cord, ribbon and twisted or braided wires—in fact, anything to which a jump ring or hook cannot be attached.

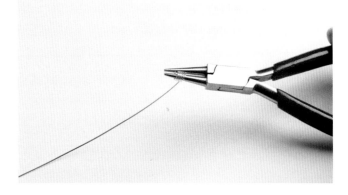

1. Working from the spool, make two coils of wire about ¼ in. long, in the same way as when making jump rings (see page 16).

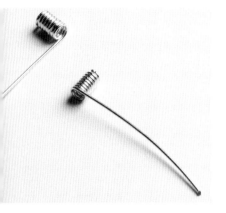

2. Cut the wire off the spool, leaving a 1-in. tail of wire on one coil and a 1½-in. tail on the other.

3. At the end of the longer wire, form a fish-hook clasp (see page 18) without a suspension link. Using your flat-nose pliers, turn the hook at 90° to the coil.

4. At the end of the shorter wire, form the eye of the fastener—again without a suspension link.

The completed coiled fish-hook clasp and fastener. If you wish, for added security, you can put a tiny dab of superglue on the end of the cord before you insert it into the coil.

5. Insert the cord or ribbon into the coil. Using your flat-nose pliers, press the last ring of the coil tightly against the cord so that the fastener is held securely in place.

Work-hardening

To create functional wire jewelry without the aid of solder, you must know how to work-harden, or toughen, your material. One effective method is to hammer the piece on a steel stake. The stake must be clean, smooth, and dent free, or the wire will pick up irregularities.

Place your piece on the stake and "stroke" hammer it, ensuring that the flat part of the hammer comes down at 90° to the piece. It is easiest to hammer standing up, as the hammer head will hit the wire squarely, rather than at an angle, which could creating texturing and "dimples" in the metal. After hammering the piece several times, you will see the wire flattening and spreading.

Be very careful when work-hardening colored wire as the colored coating can rub off, exposing the copper core.

Note that this technique is not suitable for small jump rings and links, as it will distort their shape.

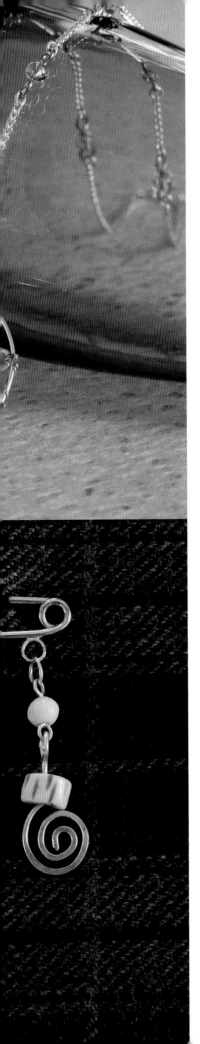

chapter 1
rings & pins

The Celts commonly used pins to fasten their cloaks and shawls. Such brooches were usually made of bronze, with one piece of metal at the head, hammered and drawn into a long wire to form a spring and pin. These pins were often decorated with semiprecious stones, beads, and coral.

In this chapter, I have provided an eclectic mix of projects, taking my inspiration from artefacts found in burial sites as well as details from illuminated manuscripts. I am sure you will enjoy creating the rings and pins for yourself and as gifts for friends and family.

spiral ring

You will need

18- and 20-gauge silver wire

3–5 semi-precious stone chips

Cylindrical dowel or ring mandrel

Round- and flat-nose pliers

Wire cutters

BELOW

The amethyst and rose quartz stone chips used on this ring are symbolic of healing, love, and harmony.

This ring design is a combination of semiprecious stones that would have been around in Celtic times and characteristic whirling spirals. It can be made with any combination of stones. Why not make one as a birthday gift, using the recipient's birthstone? I used only a few stones, as I wanted the spirals to be visible, but you could cover the entire surface with semiprecious stone chips if you wish.

1. Depending on how big you want the front of the ring to be, wrap 18-gauge silver wire four to six times around a cylindrical dowel or ring mandrel to form a coil. The dowel should be one size smaller than you want the final ring to be, as the coil will spring open slightly.

2. Cut the wire off the spool. Using the tips of your round-nose pliers, curl a little loop at each end of the coil. Holding the wire firmly with your flat-nose pliers, form each loop into a tight spiral (see page 15), curling the wires in opposite directions.

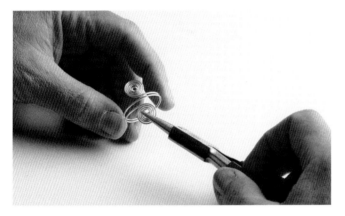

3. Continue until only one coil of wire is left between the spirals. Try and ensure that the spirals are the same diameter and meet at the same point of the coil, one above the other. Using the tips of your round-nose pliers, pull up the central loop of each spiral, so that the loops sit at right angles to the flat spirals.

4. Cut a 3–4-in. length of 20-gauge silver wire. Feed one end through one of the loops and, using your flat-nose pliers, wrap it around the loop.

5. Thread 3–5 semi-precious stone chips onto the wire, varying the shades and sizes to suit your taste. Secure the free end of the wire on the central loop of the second spiral and pull it taut, so that the chip stones are held firmly in place. Cut off any excess wire and neaten the ends (see page 17).

bead-set ring

You will need

20-gauge silver wire

4 mm round bead of your choice

Cylindrical dowel or ring mandrel

Round- and flat-nose pliers

Wire cutters

Superglue

I took my inspiration for this ring from the decoration on Celtic shields. Shell, amber, and coral were often used in Celtic shields and sword scabbards, as well as red glass or "enamel," which was made out of cuprous oxide crystals. The crystals were used in small lumps which, when softened by heat, were then shaped into small pellets or beads and secured on keyed surfaces or framed as decoration.

OPPOSITE

The bead in the center of the ring is held firmly inside a small coil of silver wire and provides a jewelike splash of color in an otherwise monochrome design.

1. Wrap 20-gauge silver wire three to four times around a cylindrical dowel or ring mandrel to form a coil. The dowel should be one size smaller than you want the final ring to be, as the coil will spring open slightly.

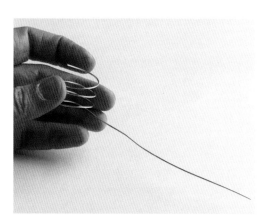

2. Pull the coil off the mandrel and cut the wire off the spool, leaving about 5 in. extending.

3. Using your fingers, twist the short, cut end of wire around the coil to hold all the loops of the coil together and form the shank of the ring. Cut off any excess wire and neaten the end (see page 17).

LEFT

Silver rings set with yellow, red, turquoise, and green beads. This design is simple to make, yet looks effective with any size of bead. Experiment with larger beads and coils of wire to obtain a more chunky effect.

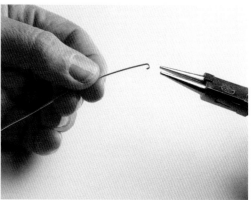

4. Using the tips of your round-nose pliers, make a small hook at the end of the extending wire.

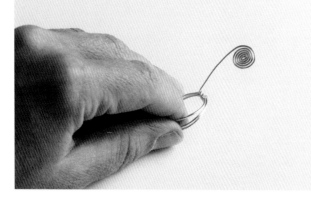

5. Using your flat-nose pliers, squeeze this hook flat to double it and continue curling it around in concentric circles, holding it flat between your pliers to form a tight spiral.

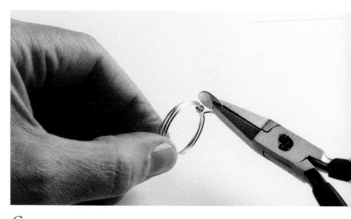

6. When the spiral meets the ring shank, fold the spiral over so that it sits at right angles to the ring shank and hides the wrapped wires that lie underneath.

7. Working from the spool, form a coil of wire around the shaft of your round-nose pliers (just as you would when creating jump rings—see page 16) that fits the diameter of the bead you have chosen to set. Coil it to the depth of the bead.

8. Cut the wire off the spool, leaving about 1 in. extending. Using your flat-nose pliers, spiral this extending wire inward, toward the coil, until it sits neatly at the base of the wire coil.

9. Push the spiral flat against the coil, so that it fills in the end of the coil.

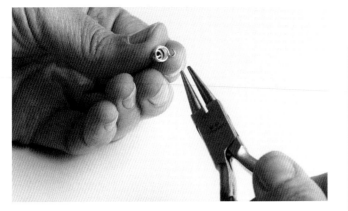

10. Curl the other cut end of the coil into a small, tight spiral, and flatten it against the side of the coil to prevent it from catching on the wearer's clothing.

11. Push the bead into the coil. (If you wish, you can put a tiny dab of Superglue inside the coil to make sure the bead is fixed in place.) Glue the spiral-and-bead unit to the center of the spiral on the ring.

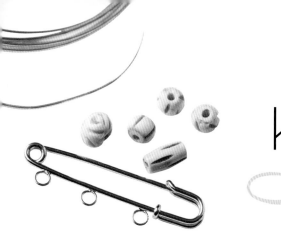

kilt pin

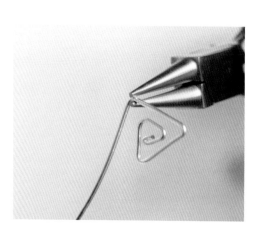

OPPOSITE

The central "cross" motif gives this pin a Celtic feel, together with the triangular and circular shaped spirals on each side. If you prefer, balance the design by making the two spirals identical.

The pin was used as a dress fastening during the Iron Age and Celtic period, and this modern-day pin can be used in the same way to secure a shawl, cardigan, skirt, or sarong. My design features a simple wire cross as the central motif, along with a spiral, which is so characteristic of Celtic style, and a triangular motif that reflects the geometric designs found on wood carvings, shields, and swords.

I used bone-effect beads, as bone is a material that would have been readily available in Celtic times, but you could use any charm, or colored beads of your choice.

You will need

18-gauge silver wire

3 x 8 mm round bone-effect beads

1 x 6 mm barrel bone-effect bead

1 x 12 mm cylinder bone-effect bead

Round- and flat-nose pliers

Wire cutters

Hammer and flat steel stake

Ready-made kilt-pin finding

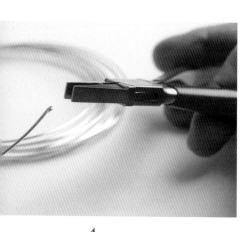

1. First make the triangular wire motif. Using the tips of your round-nose pliers, make a little hook at the end of a spool of 18-gauge silver wire. Squeeze the hook flat with your flat-nose pliers to make a head pin (see page 14).

2. Place the tips of your round-nose pliers next to this head pin, and bend the wire through 90°. Repeat five or six times, folding the wire just past the previous bend each time, to create a triangular shape.

3. Place your flat-nose pliers in the last bend, and bend the wire upward to form a stem at the top of the triangle. Cut the wire off the spool, leaving about $^1/_2$ in., and make a suspension link at the top of the motif (see page 13).

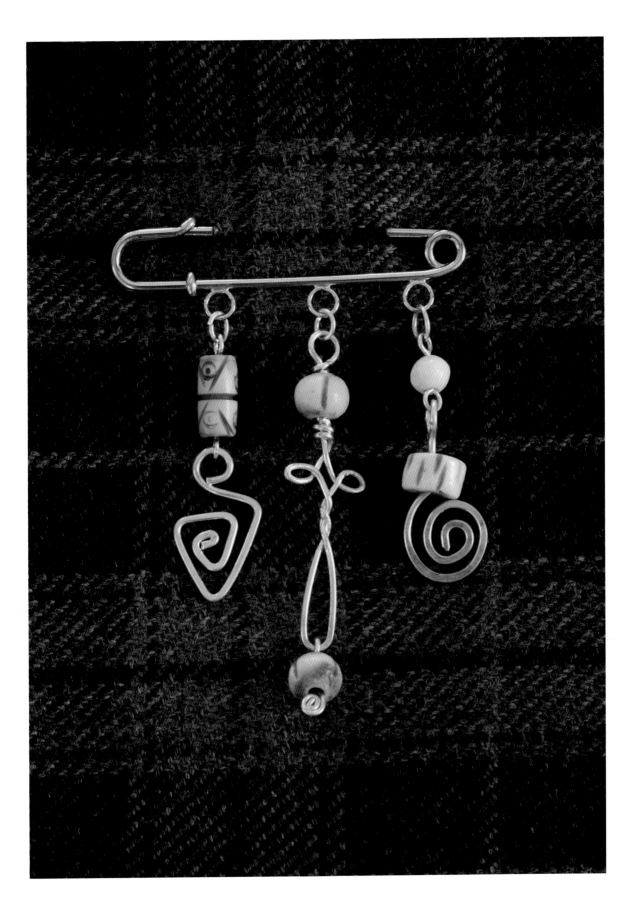

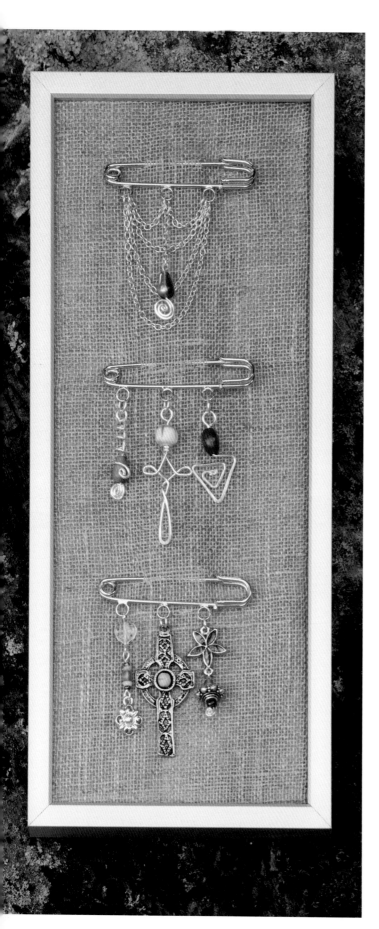

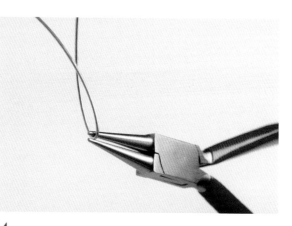

4. To make the central cross motif, cut a 6-in. length of 18-gauge silver wire. Find the center of the wire with your round-nose pliers and bring the two ends together, crossing the ends over one another about 1 in. up the wire.

5. Hammer the base of the doubled end of the wire on a steel stake to flatten it.

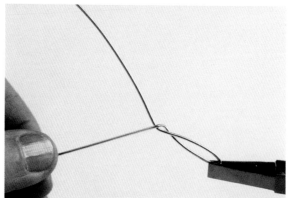

6. Twist one piece of wire around the other, just above the hammered area, to form a small loop, which will be the top of the cross motif.

OPPOSITE, FAR LEFT
Kilt pin brooches with various pendant charms— swagged chain lengths, beads, and ready-made charms. Make brooches to suit your particular style and personality.

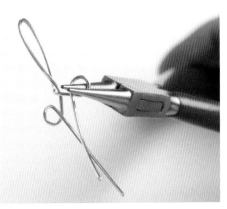

7. Place the fattest part of your round-nose pliers on one side of the twist and form a circle, curling outward, bringing the extending wire back toward the center. Repeat on the other side to form the two "arms" of the cross. Bring the two loose ends together and wrap one around the other. Cut off any excess wire and neaten the ends (see page 17).

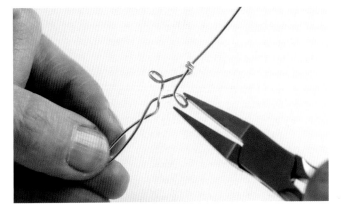

8. Squeeze the circular loops on each side of the cross with your flat-nose pliers to elongate and flatten them.

9. Thread your chosen bead onto the top of the "cross" and, using your round-nose pliers, form a suspension link (see page 13) on the projecting wire. Cut off any excess and neaten the ends (see page 17).

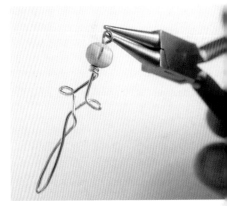

10. Working from the spool of 18-gauge silver wire, make an open spiral by curling the wire around itself (see page 15). Cut the wire off the spool, leaving about 1 in. extending. Thread your chosen bead onto the extending wire and, using your round-nose pliers, form a suspension link at the top (see page 13).

11. Thread your chosen beads onto the wires extending from the triangular and cross motifs, and form a suspension link at each end (see page 13). Make jump rings (see page 16), and attach the charms to a ready-made kilt pin.

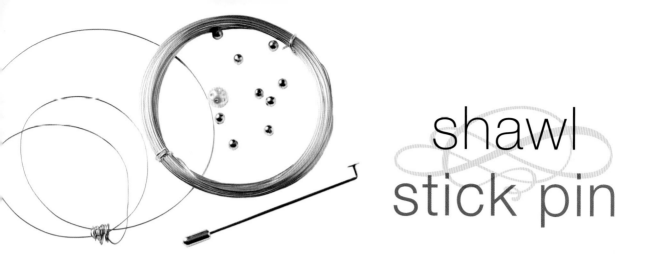

shawl
stick pin

The decorative design of this shawl or hat pin is derived from the Canna Cross—a carved stone cross on the Scottish Hebridean island of Canna, dating from between 700 and 800 CE. Although very little of it now remains, the center of the cross is in the form of a circle, representing the cycle of life. Here, I've shaped the cross using a jig, in order to be sure of making it symmetrical. The same motif also makes an attractive necklace pendant or earrings.

You will need

1 x 7 mm pearl focal bead

9 x 4 mm gold beads

20 and 28-gauge silver wire

28-gauge gold wire

Ready-made stick-pin finding with safety end

Jig and 8 small and 1 medium pegs

Jig pattern on page 124

Round- and flat-nose pliers

Wire cutters

Cylindrical dowel 1–1½ in. in diameter

Masking tape

1. Referring to the pattern on page 124, place the pegs in the jig. Wrap 10 in. of 20-gauge silver wire around the pegs, following the pattern. Carefully remove the unit from the jig, and gently tap the edges with a hammer on a steel stake to flatten them. Be careful not to hammer any crossed-over wires, as this will weaken them. Spend a little time straightening and rearranging the unit into shape, using your flat-nose pliers and fingers.

2. Wrap 20-gauge silver wire around a cylinder 1—1½ in. in diameter, making sure the wires overlap a little. Cut the wire off the spool.

Here, the shawl pin unit is suspended from a ready-made chain, with threaded beads interspersed along the chain at regular intervals to create a decorative pendant necklace design.

3. At the point where they overlap, bind the cut ends of the circle with a tiny piece of masking tape. This will form a "frame" for the cross unit.

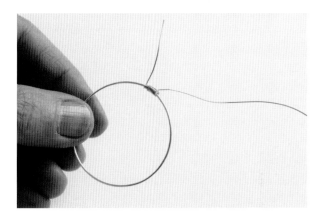

4. Cut 3–4 in. of 28-gauge gold wire. Bind this wire around the taped area of the silver-wire frame and the top two circles of the cross to attach the cross to the inside of the frame.

5. Bind the other three extremities of the cross to the frame in the same way, until it is firmly attached.

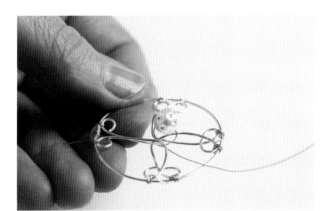

6. Cut 5 in. of 28-gauge silver wire, thread it through the center of the cross, and attach the focal bead.

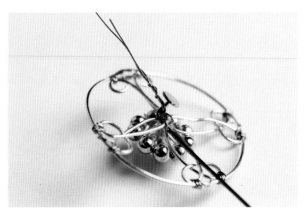

7. Thread the smaller beads around the perimeter of the central bead and secure the wire at the back of the cross.

8. Push a ready-made stick-pin finding through the back of the cross, behind the central beads, and wrap any loose wires around it to secure the finding in place.

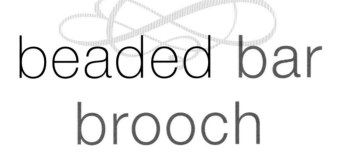

beaded bar brooch

It is almost impossible to make an exact duplicate of this design, so just let your hands flow as you thread and bend the wire into twists and wiggles. The bar-pin brooch was commonly used in Celtic times as a dress fastening and to secure shawls. Today, it makes an eye-catching piece to complement a favorite jacket or cardigan. Note that you must use sterling-silver wire for this project, as you need to file the point of the pin; if you used enamel-coated copper wire, the core would be visible after filing.

You will need

Selection of green beads and small "pearls" 3–7 mm in diameter

20-gauge sterling-silver wire

Round- and flat-nose pliers

Wire cutters

Flat needle file

Sandpaper

OPPOSITE
This brooch was made using a mix of transparent glass and opaque pearl beads, with the flowing line of the wire unifying the piece.

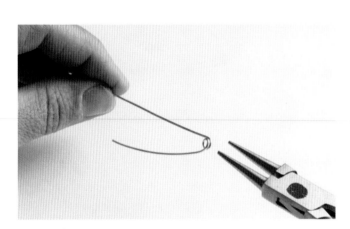

1. Cut a 10-in. length of 20-gauge sterling-silver wire. Place your round-nose pliers approximately 2 in. from one end, and twist the wire around the shaft of the pliers to curl it around in a complete loop, bringing the two ends of wire back to face in the same direction. (It should look like the end of a safety pin.)

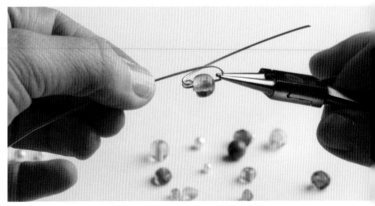

2. Thread a bead onto the longer of the two wires and push it up to the looped end. Using your round-nose pliers, bend the wire back at 180°, just beyond the bead hole.

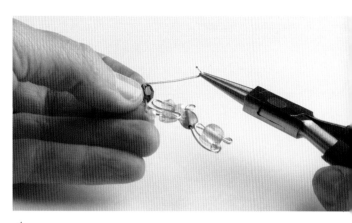

3. Continue threading beads and bending the wire into wiggly shapes in a free-form manner to create your clasp. The number of beads that you thread on is entirely up to you. If you're using relatively large beads, bend the wire after every bead. With smaller beads, thread on two or three before bending the wire.

4. Leave about 2 in. of wire projecting at the end, and then use the very tips of your round-nose pliers to bend the last ¼ in. of the wire into a hook.

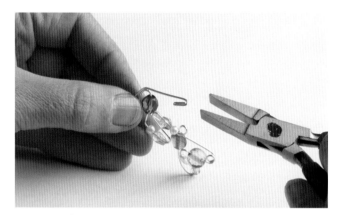

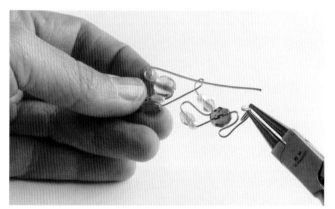

5. Squeeze the two strands of this doubled-over wire together with your flat-nose pliers. Fold the wire once more, and squeeze the doubled-over section together again with your flat-nose pliers.

6. Using the tips of your round-nose pliers, bend this folded wire up at right angles and then bend the top section at right angles again to make a small hook.

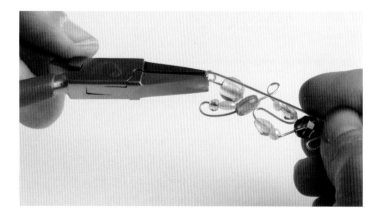

7. Straighten the wire pin (the section not threaded with beads) by stretching and pulling it out while holding the other end firmly in your flat-nose pliers. Cut off any excess, as the pin only needs to extend just past the hook fastener. Twist the doubled loop from Step 1 up through 90° so that it's at right angles to the beaded section.

BELOW
Experiment with different sizes and colors of beads—or try making bead pendant drops to suspend from the wire, as in the purple brooch shown below.

8. File the very end of the pin to a point and sandpaper the end for a smooth finish.

9. Adjust the beads and structure of the brooch with your fingers until you are satisfied with the overall shape.

chapter 2
bangles &
bracelets

Bracelets and bangles were very popular with the Celts and were worn both by men and women. The torque, which is normally in the form of a solid collar or neck ring, often created out of twisted strands of metal, is particularly associated with the Celts.

All the projects in this chapter can be extended and made as chokers and necklaces, simply by increasing the amount of wire that you use. I have also tried to introduce a mixture of colored wires to illustrate how a classical and timeless design can look thoroughly up to date when made in brightly colored wire combinations.

looped knotwork bracelet

You will need

8 x 6 mm round blue beads

8 x size 8 white seed beads

20-gauge silver wire

Round- and flat-nose pliers

½ -in. round dowel or mandrel

Hammer and steel stake

Wire cutters

Celtic warriors dyed their bodies with a substance called woad (a blue wood dye), drawing swirling patterns, much like tattoos, all over their skin to make them look fierce in battle. This bracelet was inspired by both the blue dye and those swirling patterns.

OPPOSITE

This is a simple, yet effective chain-unit design that can be created with, or without, beads. You could also try making it using two different tones of wire.

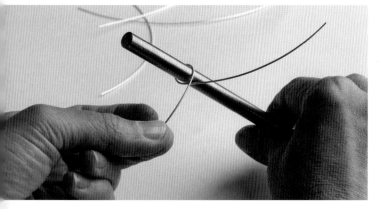

1. Cut eight 5-in. lengths of 20-gauge wire. Place your dowel or mandrel about 2 in. along the wire, and curl the wire around it to form a complete circle. (If you haven't got a mandrel, a round-barreled pen about ½ in. in diameter will do.)

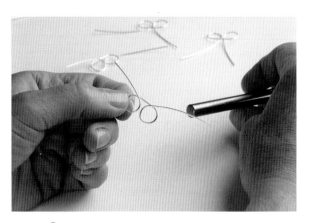

2. Place the mandrel just next to this circle of wire and curl the wire around it in the opposite direction, to form a second circle next to the first.

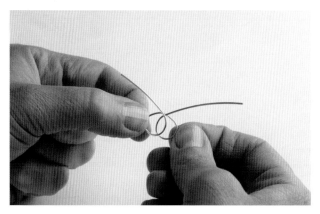

3. Using your fingers, push the two circles together so that they overlap in the center and pull the extending wires up, bringing them carefully together.

LEFT
Use the knotwork unit to make a matching set of earrings, necklace, and bracelet.

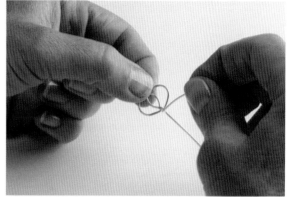

4. Using your fingers, wrap the shorter end of wire around the longer end. Cut off any excess and neaten the ends (see page 17).

5. Gently hammer and flatten the outer frame on a steel stake, being careful not to tap across any wires that overlap each other, as this will weaken them. Repeat Steps 1 through 5 to make a total of eight looped units.

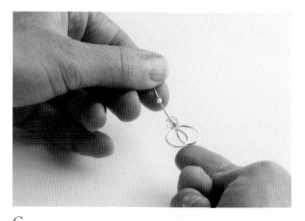

6. Thread one blue bead and one white seed bead onto the extending wire.

7. Using your round-nose pliers, form a link at the top of each unit (see page 13) at right angles to the flattened "knot."

8. Open up the link, hook the flattened wires of the "knot" of another unit over it, and then close the link with your flat-nose pliers. Connect seven units together in this way to make a chain.

9. On the eighth unit, bend the wire above the bead to form a loop, leaving about ¼ in. of wire extending.

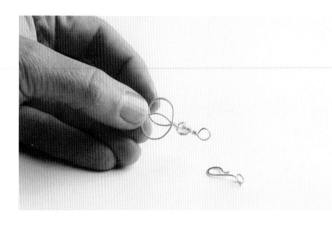

10. Wrap the extending wire around the stem. Cut off any excess wire and neaten the end (see page 17). Make a fish-hook clasp for the other end of the bracelet (see page 18).

BELOW
Here, the necklace unit has been made on a larger scale, with a spiral wire terminal added below the suspended bead for extra ornamentation.

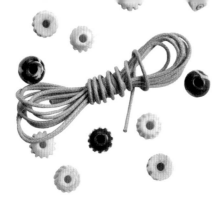

valentine knot
bracelet

No book of jewelry projects would be complete without a heart, the symbol of love, among the designs. In this bracelet, I've given the heart a very Celtic rendering with curling spirals, and have used bone- and wood-effect beads and cotton cord to reflect the materials that would have been available in those ancient times.

You will need

20-gauge silver wire

¼-in. natural cotton cord

8 x 8 mm wood- and bone-effect beads

Round- and flat-nose pliers

Wire cutters

Hammer and steel stake

Superglue (optional)

LEFT
The interlaced natural cotton cord and bone and wood beads give this bracelet a casual, informal feel. For a more jazzy effect, make it with colored wire hearts and glass beads.

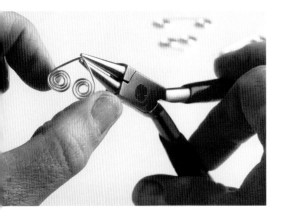

1. Cut seven 5-in. lengths of 20-gauge silver wire. Make a small loop at each end of the wire, and then form tight spirals, curling them in toward each other and leaving about ½ in. uncurled in the center of the wire. Place the tips of your round-nose pliers at the center of the wire, and push both spirals together with your fingers until they touch and form a heart shape.

2. Gently hammer each heart on a steel stake to flatten and work-harden it (see page 21). If the spirals separate, gently push them back together again with your flat-nose pliers.

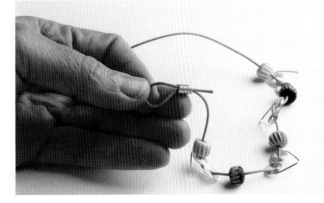

3. Thread a bone-effect bead onto ¼-in. cotton cord, then thread the cord through the holes at the top of the spirals of one wire heart, weaving it in and out as shown. Continue until all the hearts have been threaded onto the cord, alternating bone- and wood-effect beads.

4. Wrap 20-gauge silver wire around the shaft of your round-nose pliers and make a coil about ¼ in. long. Thread the coil onto the end of the cord, double it back to form a loop, and push it all the way back through the coil to secure. Using your flat-nose pliers, squeeze the last ring of the coil to keep the cord in place. Cut off any excess cord.

5. Make a coiled fish-hook clasp from 20-gauge wire (see page 20), and attach it to the other end of the cord to complete your fastening. You can add a little glue around the fastener for extra security if you wish.

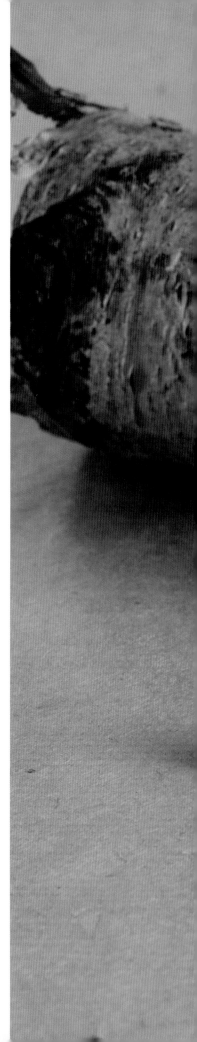

pebble and shell charm bracelet

Although no charm bracelets dating back to the Celtic era survive, I am sure that shells and natural objects would have been made into necklaces and bracelets, as the Celts were very fond of decorating and adorning themselves for ceremonial rituals. This bracelet demonstrates how you can attach un-drilled, semiprecious stones or small pebbles to a chain to create a highly individual bracelet.

You will need

24- and 20-gague gold-plated wire

6-in. ready-made gold-plated chain

14 x semiprecious "pebbles" and 13 pre-drilled shells

Round- and flat-nose pliers

Wire cutters

OPPOSITE

The gold wire enhances the warm tones of the semiprecious stone "pebbles" and shells. For a "cooler" effect, try using light blue and gray stones and silver wire.

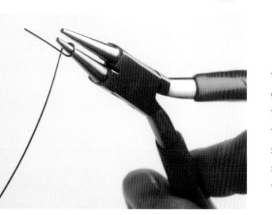

1. Place your round-nosed pliers 1 in. from the end of a spool of 24-gauge gold-plated wire. Wrap the wire around the shaft of the pliers to form a loop, then wrap the short end of the wire several times around the wire from the spool, just as when making the eye of a fastener. Cut off any excess and neaten (see page 17).

For an unusual variation on the basic design, suspend feathers, shells, and shell buttons from braided rattail ribbon. Seed pods and glass beads can also look very effective!

2. Hold the loop against the top of the pebble that you want to encase and pull the rest of the wire down the length of the pebble and back up to the top.

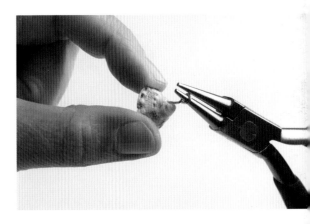

3. Wrap the wire two or three times around the pebble as tightly as you can, bringing it back to the top loop to finish. Wrap the end of the wire around the stem, just under the top loop, to secure and cut it off the spool with your wire cutters. Neaten the end (see page 17).

4. Cut about 1 in. of 24-gauge gold-plated wire, and thread it through a pre-drilled shell. Form a head pin at one end and a link at the other (see pages 13 and 14).

5. Make 27 jump rings and a fish-hook clasp and eye from 20-gauge gold-plated wire (see pages 16, 18, and 20). Attach the clasp and eye to the ends of the bracelet. Suspend the pebbles and shells from the chain, using the jump rings.

braided wire
bangle

You will need

Three colors of 20-gauge wire

Masking tape

Round-and flat-nose pliers

Wire cutters

Vise

Cylindrical dowel or mandrel, 2 in. in diameter

Superglue (optional)

The interlacing knots in Celtic designs are meant to mean "everlasting," as there are no beginnings or ends, and braiding is perhaps the simplest form of interlacing. Try experimenting with braiding different-colored wires, threading beads on alternate braids, or braiding a mixture of wire, ribbon, and leather. You'll be amazed at the variety of designs you can create!

1. Cut nine 6-in. lengths of 20-gauge wire, three of each color. Place them together in three groups of three, with one wire of each color in each group, and bind the ends with masking tape. Secure the taped end in the vise, and braid the wires together, keeping the wires flat and the colors in sequence (see page 17). Remove from the vise and bind the untaped end with masking tape to hold the braid together.

LEFT

Vary the design by adding beads, replacing one of the wires with cord, or twisting wires together before braiding them and adding a bead-and-spiral terminal.

2. Shape the braided bangle around a dowel or mandrel. (If you haven't got a mandrel, you could use a small jar or can.)

3. Make two coils of 20-gauge wire about ½ in. long, in the same way as when making jump rings (see page 16). Cut the wire off the spool, leaving about 1 in. extending. Curl the projecting ends of the coils into tight spirals (see page 15), then push them up flat against the coils to fill in the ends.

4. Slip the coils over the ends of the bangle to cover the taped, cut wires and secure by squeezing the last ring tightly against the braided wire with your flat-nose pliers. If you wish, you can put a tiny dab of superglue inside the coil for extra security.

twisted
torque bangle

You will need

Six colors of 20-gauge wire

4 x 5mm round silver beads

Masking tape

Round- and flat-nose pliers

Wire cutters

Vise and hand drill

Cylindrical dowels or mandrels,
¼ in. and 2 in. in diameter

The most beautiful torque bracelets and neck rings have been recovered from Celtic burial sites. The torque was a badge of rank and power, and classical writers have reported that Queen Boadicea wore a golden neck ring and bangles when she went into battle against the Romans. This technique can be used to make a variety of choker collars, as well as bangles, and beads can be introduced to plug the ends of the wire.

BELOW
The bracelet and choker neck-ring torque look fun and jazzy made in these bright colored wires. For a more classic, elegant look, use a combination of gold and silver wires.

1. Cut six 14-in. lengths of 20-gauge colored wire, one in each color, tape the ends with masking tape, and twist together (see page 17). Remove the wires from the drill and vise. Wrap the twisted wires loosely around a cylindrical dowel mandrel 2 in. in diameter, and form into a circle.

2. Remove the masking tape from the ends of the twisted wires. Place the small dowel or mandrel about 2 in. from one end and curl the twisted wires around it to form a loop. Repeat at the other end of the bangle, coiling this loop in the opposite direction to the first one.

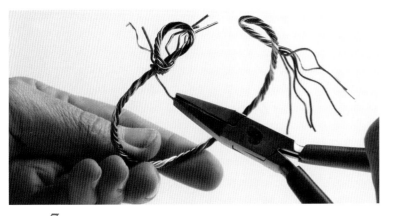

3. Unravel the ends of the twisted wires on both sides up to the point at which the loop begins. Push three wires behind the loop on each side, and three in front of it. Wrap two of the wires in front of the loop around the bangle several times, cut off any excess, and neaten the ends (see page 17).

4. Form the remaining wire in front of the loop into a tight spiral (see page 15), and press it flat against the wires that you wrapped around the bangle in the previous step to hide them.

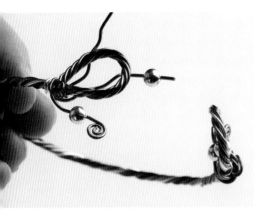

5. Form one of the remaining wires on each side into a spiral (see page 15). Thread one silver bead onto the two remaining wires on each side, and spiral the ends (see page 15).

6. Adjust the positions of the spirals and beads with your fingers, so that they can be seen through the loops.

chapter 3
spiral chains

The spiral is probably the most characteristic and distinctive symbol of the Celtic style. In this chapter, you will learn how to create spiral units to form beautiful, hand-made chains that reflect the timeless, swirling patterns of the ancient craftsmen. Experiment with using other gauges and types of wire than those suggested here; you will be surprised at how different the results can look!

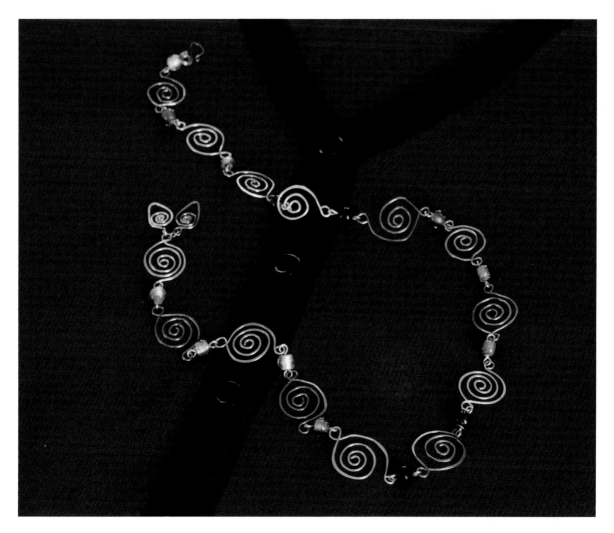

The spiral is perhaps the most identifiable shape of Celtic culture and this chain is the epitome of Celtic style. The Irish Celts used the spiral as a symbol of their sun. A loosely wound spiral, as in this design, meant a big sun and was the symbol for "summer," while a tightly wound spiral, as in the Double Spiral Necklace on page 62, stood for "winter." Make this chain in a classic gold-and-silver combination or, for a summery, contemporary look, use a blend of colored wires.

open spiral
bracelet

ABOVE

The open spirals of gold and silver wire are interspersed with colored beads to produce a necklace that can be linked at varying heights between the spirals.

You will need

20-gauge gold and silver wire

Round- and flat-nose pliers

Wire cutters

Hammer and steel stake

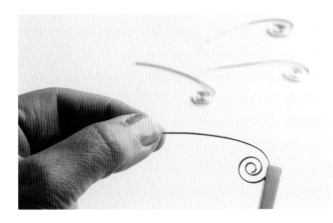

1. Cut four 4-in. lengths of 20-gauge gold wire and three of silver. Using the tips of your round-nose pliers, curl a small loop at one end of each piece of wire. Holding this loop tightly in your flat-nose pliers, form the wire into an open spiral (see page 15).

2. When you have about 2 in. of wire left, place your round-nose pliers on the wire and curl it around in the opposite direction to the spiral to form a small loop.

3. Hold the small loop in your flat-nose pliers and pull the extending wire around the outside of the open spiral.

4. Using the tips of your round-nose pliers, curl the end of the extending wire back on itself to form a second loop on the opposite side.

5. Hammer each spiral to flatten and work-harden it (see page 21).

6. Make seven silver jump rings (see page 16), and link the spirals together, alternating gold and silver units. To complete the bracelet, make a spiral clasp (see page 18).

double spiral
necklace

This double spiral is less delicate than the Open Spiral Bracelet on page 60. Each unit is made from one piece of doubled-over wire, providing a very solid, metallic effect. For an elegant matching set, make earrings from just one double spiral, suspended with a pendant bead.

You will need

20-gauge copper wire

20-gauge silver wire

Round- and flat-nose pliers

Wire cutters

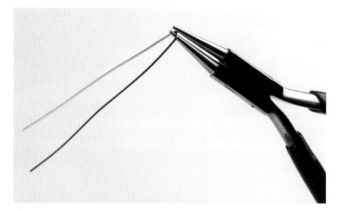

1. Cut six 6-in. lengths of 20-gauge silver wire and twelve of copper. Bend each length in half by placing the tips of your round-nose pliers in the center and pulling and straightening the wire on each side so that it runs straight and parallel.

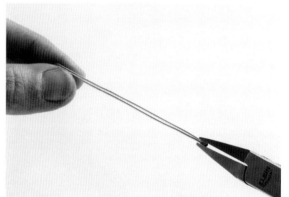

2. Using your flat-nose pliers, squeeze the doubled wires together so that they run parallel to each other.

3. Using the tips of your round-nose pliers, curl the doubled end into a hook, making sure that the wires remain parallel to one another and do not overlap.

OPPOSITE
The double-spiral units can be linked into attractive necklace chains using any colored wire combinations. For a lighter effect, intersperse beads or coiled wire spacers between the spirals (top).

LEFT
*Two silver jump rings
connect the copper and silver
spiral units together and
help to balance the design.*

4. Using your flat-nose pliers, curl the doubled wires into a tight spiral until you are left with about ½ in. of wire.

5. Separate the projecting wires and, using your round-nose pliers, curl the bottom wire into a link (see page 13).

6. Curl the top projecting wire into another link, curling it around your round-nose pliers until it sits opposite the first link. Cut off any excess wire.

7. Make 34 jump rings from 20-gauge silver wire (see page 16). Placing two jump rings between each unit, connect the spirals together, adding one silver spiral after every two copper.

8. To complete the necklace, make a spiral clasp (see page 18) using 20-gauge silver wire.

BELOW
This close-up photograph shows the hammered spiral clasp, which reinforces the Celtic theme of the necklace and provides a tough, but decorative, finishing touch.

duo spiral bracelet

You will need

20-gauge pink wire

20-gauge green wire

Round- and flat-nose pliers

Wire cutters

Early man observed the beauty of nature's spirals, using them as a symbol of eternity, symbolizing life, death, and rebirth. Spirals can be found in the art of most early civilizations, but it was the Celts who found a way of weaving two, three, four, or even more coils together.

These fun, colorful bracelets, made from two tones of wire, can also be made in gold and silver for a more reserved, classic effect. You could also make matching earrings by suspending one or two spiral units from ready-made earwires.

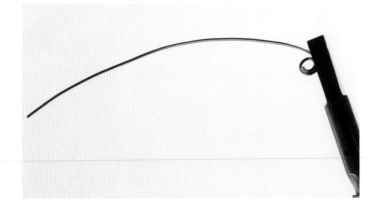

OPPOSITE

Both of these Duo Spiral Bracelets are made from two tones of colored wire— purple with dark blue, and pink with pale green. Experiment with your favorite color combinations.

1. Cut four 5-in. lengths of 20-gauge green wire and three of pink. Using your flat-nose pliers, curl a circle at one end and begin to form a tight spiral around it, holding the circle firmly in the jaws of the pliers.

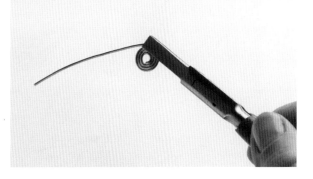

2. Continue spiraling the wire until you are about 2 in. from the end.

3. Using your round-nose pliers, curl a small loop at the end of the wire, curling it inward.

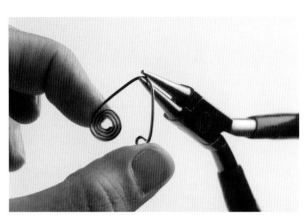

4. Place the tips of your round-nose pliers in the center of the wire, and push the spiral and loop in toward each other.

5. Holding the loop of wire firmly in your flat-nose pliers, form a tight spiral, spiraling it inward until it sits just below the larger spiral.

6. To make the clasp, cut another 5-in. length of 20-gauge pink wire. Spiral both ends in toward each other, leaving approximately 1 in. of unspiraled wire in the center.

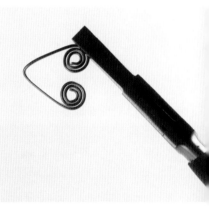

7. Place the tips of your round-nose pliers in the center of the unspiraled wire, and push the spirals together with your fingers until they overlap. Gently press the spirals together, so that they sit on top of each other.

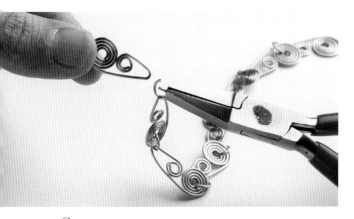

BELOW
The end clasp on the Duo Spiral Bracelet chain is a very effective and decorative way of fastening a bracelet.

8. Make eight large jump rings from green wire (see page 16), and connect the spiral units together as shown, alternating the colors.

9. Attach the clasp to one end of the bracelet.

10. Loosen the last coil of the last pink spiral. Hook it over the clasp to close the bracelet.

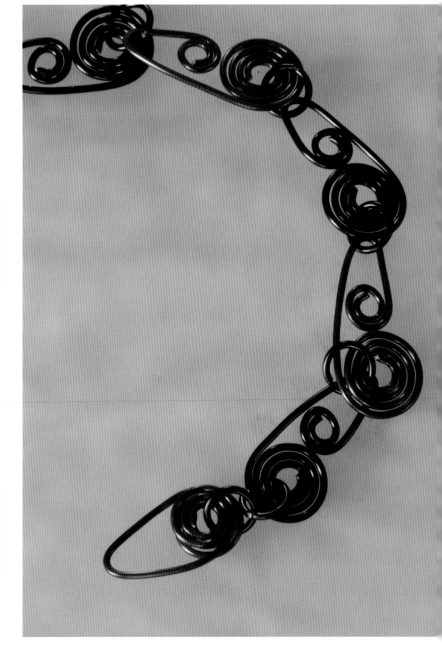

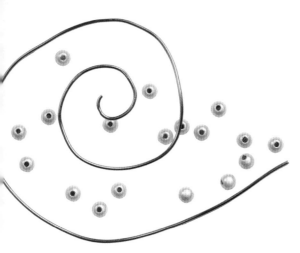

wavy chain

This chain unit has been one of my favorites for many years. Here I have given it a Celtic twist by extending the ends of the curved units into spirals.

Scotland and Ireland were the heartlands of Celtic civilization, and the coastal areas of these two countries have some of the most dramatic scenery. This design is intended to evoke the waves hitting the cliffs, with the blue-green wire representing the waves and the silver wire representing the hard granite of the rocks.

You will need

20-gauge silver wire

20-gauge green wire

24-gauge silver wire

40 x 5 mm silver beads

Round- and flat-nose pliers

Wire cutters

Cylindrical dowel 1 in. in diameter

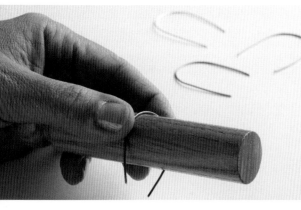

1. Cut ten 3-in. lengths of 20-gauge silver wire and ten of green. Find the center of each piece, and bend it around a cylindrical dowel to curve it into a shallow "U" shape.

2. Using the tips of your round-nose pliers, curl one end of each unit into a small circle. Thread two 5mm silver beads onto the other end of the wire.

OPPOSITE
This highly decorative chain necklace is made using two contrasting colors of wire, with pearly silver beads adding fullness to the piece. Try making the chain with smaller spirals and without beads; you'll be amazed at how different it can look!

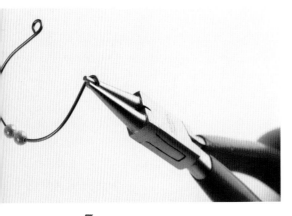

3. Curl another small circle on the other side of the curved wire.

5. Cut 21 ½-in. pieces of 24-gauge silver wire. Using the tips of your round-nose pliers, form a circle at each end of each piece, curling them in opposite directions to make a figure eight.

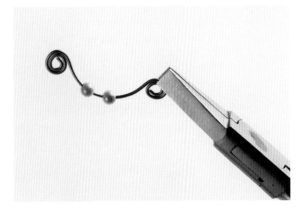

4. Form a small, tight spiral (see page 15) at each end of the wire, curling the wires inward, until you are left with about 1 in. of unspiraled wire, with the two beads at the center.

6. To join the units together, open one side of a figure eight piece and attach it to one of the green curved units, between the two beads. Attach the other side of the figure eight piece to a silver unit in the same way, making sure that both curves face inward.

7. Repeat Step 6 until you have linked all the units together and formed a chain, alternating the colors as shown.

OPPOSITE

This silver wire and gold bead version of the Wavy Chain would look stunning for a formal occasion. Alternatively, a combination of gold wire and pearls would be the perfect complement for a bridal dress.

8. To complete, make a fish-hook clasp and eye (see pages 18 and 20).

swirling chain

This decorative pattern was inspired by the border designs found on Celtic chalices, scabbard plates, and illuminated manuscripts. The chain—an apparently seamless circle of swirling spirals—has a classic, timeless quality. It is fastened by simply opening one of the loops in the last chain unit slightly and hooking it over the first chain, as I felt that a conventional hook-and-eye fastener would break the circle and disrupt the unity of the piece.

You will need

20-gauge silver wire

Round- and flat-nose pliers

Wire cutters

Hammer and steel stake

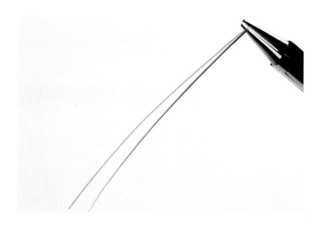

1. Cut eleven 9-in. lengths of 20-gauge silver wire. Bend each length in half by placing the tips of your round-nose pliers in the center.

OPPOSITE
These swirling silver spirals form a continuous chain necklace that would look attractive with both formal and casual clothes.

2. Squeeze the doubled-over end of wire with your flat-nose pliers, and pull the wires with your fingers so that they run straight and parallel to one another.

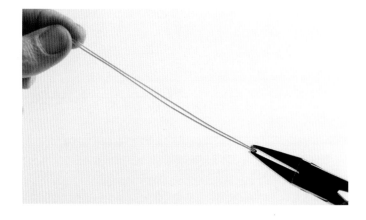

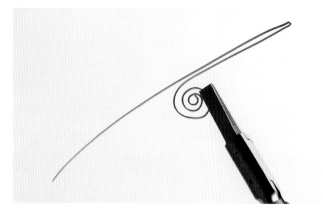

3. Using your round-nose pliers, curl one end of the wire into a circle. Hold the circle firmly in the jaws of your flat-nose pliers, then curl the wire outward into an open spiral, leaving about 1½ in. of wire unspiraled.

4. Form another open spiral on the other side, spiraling it outward as before, so that it sits just above the first.

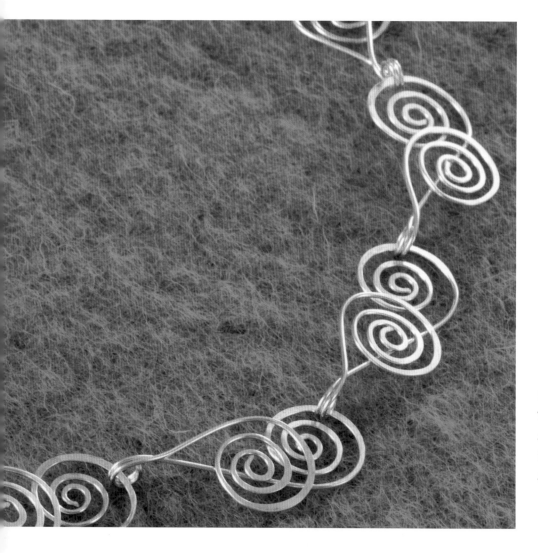

LEFT
This close-up photograph shows more clearly the interlocking system of the swirling wire units.

5. Hammer both spirals on a steel stake to flatten and work harden them (see page 21)—but take care not to hammer the doubled-over end of the wire.

6. Place the fattest part of your round-nose pliers at the end of the doubled wire and curl the wire forward, to form a complete circle at 90° to the spirals. Make this link on ten of the eleven units. On the final unit, leave the link slightly ajar as this will form the clasp.

7. Push both spirals in toward each other, so that they sit above one another. The wire is very springy, so you will need to push the top spiral just past the bottom one as it will spring back to sit in the correct position.

8. Connect all eleven units together by linking one end into the other to form a chain.

9. Hook the last unit with the slightly open link onto the last spiral to act as an invisible clasp.

chapter 4
necklaces
& chokers

As a symbol of continuity, interlacing knotwork patterns in Celtic borders and panels are an imitation of braiding and weaving, and were used as decoration for stone, wood, and metal. Pictish artist-craftsmen, in particular, concentrated on geometrical constructions, interlacing not only linear patterns, but also limbs and bodies of humans, animals, birds, and reptiles.

The projects in this chapter show how you can braid and twist wires together, as well as create interwoven structures using a jig. Even though the chapter concentrates on necklace designs, the units on each piece can be constructed in duplicate and suspended on ear wires to create matching earrings.

lindisfarne choker

When the Celts converted to Christianity and founded their monasteries, they copied Gospel text from manuscripts originally brought from Eastern Christendom, particularly Byzantine and North African Coptic churches. These highly decorative eastern influences were combined with the native flowing Celtic style, producing wonderful decorative patterns such as those found in the knotwork borders of the world-famous Lindisfarne Gospels, which inspired the pattern in this choker.

You will need

20-gauge silver wire

9 x 8 mm blue faceted beads

9 x 6 mm purple faceted beads

Round- and flat-nose pliers

Wire cutters

Hammer and steel stake

Jig and 7 small pegs

Jig pattern on page 124

OPPOSITE, TOP
Choose beads in jewelike colors—amethyst and a rich blue similar to lapis lazuli—to echo the vibrant painted decorations of the Lindisfarne Gospels.

1. Cut nine 7-in. lengths of 20-gauge silver wire. Following the pattern on page 124, place the pegs in your jig and loop the wire around them. Make nine units. Gently "stroke" hammer the units on a steel stake (see page 17), avoiding the crossed-over wires. Using your flat-nose pliers, twist the top two links of each unit through 90° so that they face each other.

2. Thread eight of the blue beads onto 20-gauge silver wire, and form a link at each end (see page 13). Now thread all nine purple beads onto 20-gauge silver wire, and form a head pin at one end (see page 14) and a link at the other.

3. Starting and ending with a wire unit, and alternating wire units and blue beads, connect all the wire units together to form a chain.

4. Using 20-gauge silver wire, make nine jump rings (see page 14), and suspend one purple bead from the link at the base of each wire unit. Make an S-clasp (see page 19), incorporating the remaining blue bead as a central feature.

You will need

- 20-gauge pink wire
- 20-gauge silver wire
- 28-gauge silver wire
- 10 mm pearl cabochon bead
- Silver elasticated cord
- Superglue
- Round- and flat-nose pliers
- Wire cutters
- Jig with 5 small, 1 medium, and 1 large peg
- Jig pattern on page 125
- Hand drill and vise
- ½-in. cylindrical dowel
- Hammer and steel stake

book of kells
choker

I took my inspiration for this choker from the Book of Kells, an illuminated manuscript now housed in the library of Trinity College, Dublin, that dates back more than 1200 years and is regarded as one of the greatest surviving treasures of Celtic art. The "stone" in this choker represents the stones from which the monks would have ground their colors. The pink wire unit represents the swirling framework and lavish ornamentation of the illuminated text.

2. Gently flatten the wire unit on a steel stake with a hammer, being very careful not to remove the color coating on the wire. Repeat Steps 1 and 2 to make a second unit.

1. Cut two 7-in. lengths of 20-gauge pink wire. Following the pattern on page 124, place the pegs in your jig. Using your round-nose pliers, form a loop at one end of the first length of wire and pull it tightly around the first peg. Now loop the wire around the remaining pegs, following the pattern. Snip off any excess wire.

3. Using your flat-nose pliers, twist the top two links through 90°, so that they face each other.

This choker would look great with any outfit, from jeans to an elegant ball gown! To make matching earrings, simply suspend a pearl bead in the center of the base loop, and attach the unit to ready-made earwires.

LEFT

In these red and green variations, black cotton cord gives a more informal look. Matching earrings complete the sets, with the suspended beads encased in wire as in the Charm Cascade Clip on page 108.

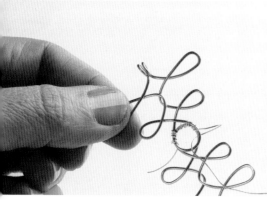

4. Cut a 3-in. length of 28-guage silver wire. Place the two larger circles of the units on top of one another, and wrap the wire around to bind them together.

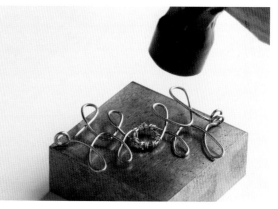

5. Flatten the bound area by gently hammering on a steel stake. Cut off any excess wire and neaten the ends (see page 17).

6. Twist three 5-in. lengths of 20-gauge silver wire together using a vise and hand drill (see page 17). Wrap the twisted wire twice around a dowel ½ in. in diameter.

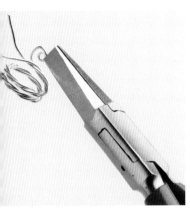

7. Remove the masking tape from one end of the twisted wire. Untwist about 2 in. of the wires. Using your flat-nose pliers, curl each one into an open spiral (see page 15).

8. Pull the spirals over the central hole of the twisted wire frame to form a base for the bead.

9. Place the cabochon stone in the center of the twisted wire frame. Untwist about 2 in. of the wires at the other end of the frame. Using your flat-nose pliers, begin curling each one into an open spiral (see page 15), and place the stone in the center.

10. Spiral the remaining ends of each wire, and press and flatten the spirals over the cabochon stone to hold it in place. Glue the framed cabochon stone to the center of the pink unit.

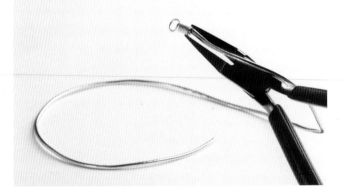

11. Using your round-nose pliers, make two ¼-in. coils of 20-gauge silver wire, as when making jump rings (see page 16). Cut the wire off the spool, leaving 1 in. at each end. Form a link at each end (see page 13).Thread one coil onto each end of a length of elasticated cord. Squeeze the end ring of the coil tightly around the cord to secure.

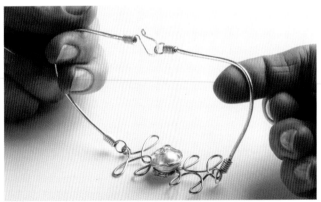

12. Cut the cord in half. Undo the link at each end of the decorated unit, attach to the links on the elasticated cord, and close up the links with your flat-nose pliers. To complete the necklace, make a coiled fish-hook clasp (see page 20), and attach it to the ends.

triskele choker

OPPOSITE

Suspend the triskele motif from a twisted-wire choker ring made from the same two colors of wire, as here, or from a ready-made chain or ribbon.

The triskele, or triskelion, is a motif consisting of three interlocking spirals. Three-piece spirals were used by the early monks, probably to represent the Trinity of the Father, Son, and Holy Spirit. The number three was also very important to the Celts, as it stood for the on-going cycle of birth, life, and death—so this choker has strong symbolic links to Celtic culture and history.

You will need

20-gauge pink wire

20-gauge purple wire

Round- and flat-nose pliers

Wire cutters

Jig with 5 small, 1 medium, and 1 large peg

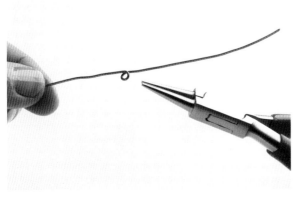

1. Cut a 6-in. length of 20-gauge pink wire. Find the center of the wire and carefully twist it around the tips of your round-nose pliers to form a little circle.

2. Curl each end of the wire into an open spiral (see page 15), curling in opposite directions like the letter "S."

3. Cut a 5-in. length of 20-gauge pink wire, and form another spiral the same diameter as the first two, leaving a tail of wire about 2 in. long.

LEFT
This detail shows clearly how the triskele motif is linked to both the circular outer frame and the twisted-wire choker ring by means of jump rings.

4. Thread this tail of wire through the central loop of the double spiral, and wrap it two or three times around the central loop to secure. You should be left with about 1½ in. of wire protruding.

5. Using your round-nose pliers, form a small loop at the end of this protruding wire. Hold the loop in your flat-nose pliers, and curl the wire into a tight spiral (see page 15). Press the spiral flat against the center of the triskele motif to hide the wrapped wires underneath. If necessary, adjust the shape of the spirals using your fingertips and flat-nose pliers.

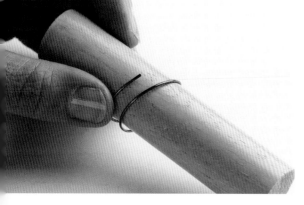

6. Wrap 20-gauge pink wire once around a circular mandrel about 1¼ in. in diameter, letting the ends overlap by about ½ in. Cut the wire off the spool.

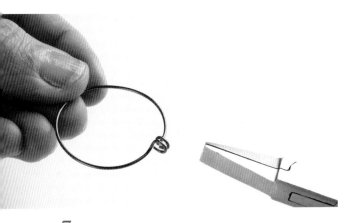

7. Using your round-nose pliers, form a link at each end (see page 13). Using your flat-nose pliers, twist the links through 90° so that they face each other.

8. Make one large and four medium-sized jump rings (see page16). Thread one medium-sized jump ring through one of the spirals of the triskele motif. Position this ring between the top two links of the circular frame. Thread another ring through both sides of the frame and the jump ring holding the motif, so that the motif is suspended at the top of the circular frame.

9. Connect the other two spirals to the frame using the remaining medium-sized jump rings.

10. Attach the triskele motif to a twisted wire choker frame or ribbon, using the large jump ring.

RIGHT
Make matching earrings, without the circular frame, and suspend them from tight spirals with earring posts glued to the back.

wrapped stone pendant

You will need

Polished stone 1¼– 1½ in. in length

20-gauge silver wire

16-in. length of black cotton cord

Round- and flat-nose pliers

Wire cutters

It is probable that the Celtic tribes would have kept stones as talismans and charms, and this project shows how you could wrap a pebble, semiprecious polished stone or, in fact, anything that does not have a drilled hole to be threaded. The next time you are on vacation, or having a weekend break, look for an interesting stone, piece of bark, or fragment of china or glass and take it home to be wrapped in wire and turned into a pendant as a souvenir of your trip.

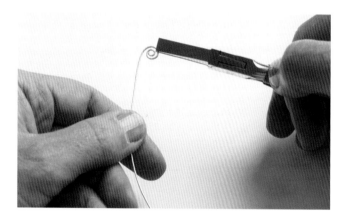

1. Cut a length of 20-gauge silver wire approximately four times the length of the stone. Curl one end into an open spiral (see page 15).

OPPOSITE

Stones of all shapes and sizes can be lightly wrapped in wire to create striking centerpieces.

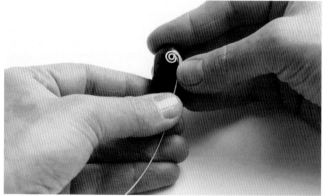

2. Hold the spiral at the top of the stone, flat against the back, and pull the wire down to the base of the stone.

3. Wrap the wire around the front and middle of the stone a couple of times, and then bring it around to the top of the front of the stone.

4. Using your fingers, uncoil the spiral at the back.

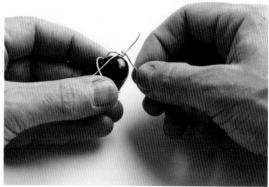

ABOVE

Here you can see an alternative version of the end clasp, which has a wire heart decoration. A spiral or threaded bead would look equally attractive.

5. Wrap the cut end of the wire around the stem to secure. Cut off any excess and neaten the ends (see page 17).

6. Using your round-nose pliers, form a link at the end of the protruding wire (see page 13). Cut off any excess wire and neaten the ends (see page 17).

7. To form the top bail of the pendant, cut a 5-in. length of 20-gauge silver wire and fold it in half, squeezing the ends together so that the doubled wires run parallel to each other.

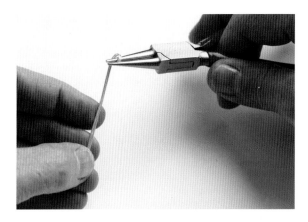

8. Using the ends of your round-nose pliers, curl the doubled-up end of wire into a loop.

9. Holding the loop in your left hand, curl a spiral at each loose end of the wire, curling the spirals outward in opposite directions.

10. Place the widest part of your round-nose pliers around the wires just past the loop, and bend the wires down to form a hook.

11. Attach the link at the top of the wrapped stone into the doubled link on the bail.

12. Thread a length of jewelry cord through the center of the bail. Make sure that the spirals are pressed firmly against the front. Make a coiled fishhook clasp and fastener for the cord (see page 20).

3-C scroll pendant

You will need

20-gauge silver wire

28-gauge silver wire

4 x 8 mm crackle-effect beads

1 x 6 mm black bead

1 x 0.5 mm crimp bead

Nylon filament

Black organza ribbon

Masking tape

Round- and flat-nose pliers

Wire cutters

I found this motif on a fragment of an Irish golden brooch dating back to the eighth or ninth century. The brooch was fabricated from beaten sheet gold, soldered with the 3-C scroll wire pattern. You can enlarge or reduce the design depending on the amount of wire and size of beads that you use. Alternatively, make it with twisted wires to create a more filigree effect.

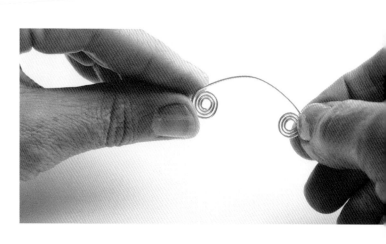

1. Cut three 6-in. lengths of 20-gauge silver wire and spiral each end inward, leaving about 1 in. of wire in the center. Make sure that the spirals are approximately the same diameter on each side.

OPPOSITE

This bold pendant design is made with crackle-effect porcelain beads suspended from an organza ribbon, but any colored beads would look effective.

2. Holding the spirals with your fingers, slightly bend each unit so that it is shaped like a shallow letter "C" or crescent.

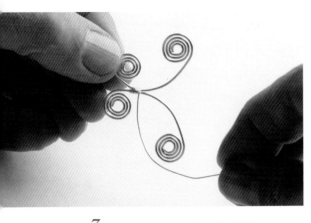

3. Cut a 2–3-in. length of 28-gauge silver wire. With the curves of the first two C-shapes facing inward, bind the first two units together just under the top two spirals.

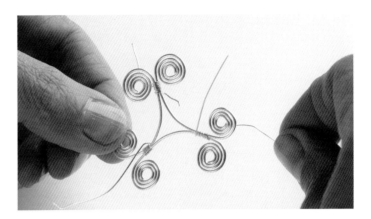

4. Cut two more pieces of 28-gauge silver wire, and attach the third unit in the same way. Cut off any excess wire and neaten the ends (see page 17).

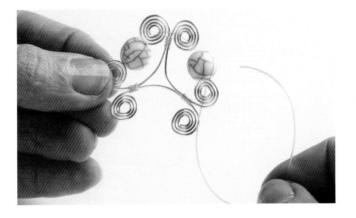

5. Cut a 4-in. length of nylon filament. Thread it through three of the crackle-effect beads and the centers of the spirals, as shown, until both ends of the filament meet at the top of the motif.

6. Keeping the nylon filament taut, thread both ends of the filament through one black, one crackle-effect, and one crimp bead. Push the nylon filament back through the crimp bead to form a loop, and then press the crimp bead with your flat-nose pliers or crimping pliers to secure. Cut off any excess filament.

7. Make two coils of 20-gauge silver wire about ¼ in. long, in the same way as when making jump rings (see page 16). Thread a length of ½-in. black organza ribbon through the first coil, then through the nylon loop, and finally through the second coil. Push both coils up tight against the nylon loop.

8. Make a coiled fish-hook clasp and fastener (see page 20), and attach to the ribbon ends.

9. To finish, squeeze the last coil with your flat-nose pliers to secure.

ABOVE

This version uses gold wire and red beads, with the motif being suspended from a gold chain interspersed with red beads. Experiment to create your own variations.

celtic cross

You will need

20-gauge silver wire

18-gauge silver wire

Selection of 2–4 mm green and transparent beads

1 x 8 mm green focal bead

24 x size 8 green seed beads

Round- and flat-nose pliers

Wire cutters

Jig and 13 small pegs

Jig pattern on page 125

Hammer and steel stake

Many of the finest examples of Celtic metalwork were created for the church, and embellished with precious and semiprecious gems. This jig pattern is a simplified, modern-day interpretation of a traditional Celtic-style cross. Celtic crosses differ from the later Christian crosses, which have a longer central stem. It is supposed that Celtic crosses were designed symmetrically to fit into a circle (the symbol of the cycle of life). My design is suspended from a hand-made chain of S-shaped units threaded with tiny seed beads, but you could use a ready-made chain if you prefer.

OPPOSITE
This elegant cross has a centerpiece of green faceted beads, suspended from a hand-made S-link chain.

1. Cut a 13-in. length of 18-gauge silver wire. Following the pattern on page 125, place the pegs in your jig. Using your round-nose pliers, form a loop at one end of the wire and pull it tightly around the first peg. Now loop the wire around the remaining pegs, following the pattern. Snip off any excess wire.

2. Remove the wire motif from the pegs, and gently "stroke" hammer the unit on a steel stake (see page 21).

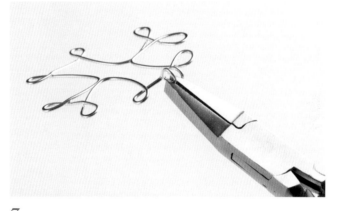

3. Using your flat-nose pliers, turn the top two links through 90° so that they face each other.

4. Lay the beads down the center of the cross to work out the arrangement. Cut a piece of 20-gauge silver wire about 1½ in. longer than the cross. Using your round-nose pliers, form a link at one end (see page 13), and thread on the beads. Using your flat-nose pliers, form a small, tight spiral at the other end of the wire (see page 15).

5. Thread the link through the top two loops of the cross, and close it with your flat-nose pliers.

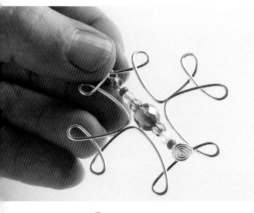

6. Bend the spiral over the base of the cross, and press firmly with your fingers to hold it in place.

7. To make a 16-in. chain, cut 24 1-in. lengths of 20-gauge silver wire. Using your round-nose pliers, form a complete circle at one end of each wire, and thread on one size 8 green seed bead. Using your round-nose pliers, form another complete circle at the other end of each wire, trapping the green bead in the center of the S-shaped unit.

8. Make 26 jump rings (see page 16) from 20-gauge silver wire. Starting and ending with a jump ring, connect twelve S-shaped units together. Repeat, using the remaining jump rings and S-shaped units.

OPPOSITE
For a more casual effect, make the cross using different colors of beads and suspend it from a braided cord choker in matching colors or from a bail, as in the Wrapped Stone Pendant on page 90.

11. Connect one end of each chain to the top link of the cross.

12. To complete the necklace, make a spiral clasp from 20-gauge wire (see page 18), and attach to the ends of the chains.

butterfly necklace

You will need

24-gauge black iron wire

Approx. 100 size 8 green and black seed beads

1 x 5 mm green wood bead

Tan, black, and green cord

Masking tape

Round- and flat-nose pliers

Wire cutters

Hammer and steel block

Vise

Superglue (optional)

OPPOSITE
Make this black-wire butterfly in your favorite colors to suit your personal style. The braided cord gives a Celtic look.

Much of Celtic art depicts animals as the subject. Even though butterflies were not as popular as dogs, horses, and roosters, I have given this piece a Celtic theme, through the beaded spirals on each wing. You could use the same motif on a brooch or hat pin, or wire the butterflies onto plant sticks, so that they can flutter amongst your pots in the garden!

1. Using your round-nose pliers, make a ¼-in. coil of 24-gauge black wire, in the same way as when making jump rings (see page 16). Holding the top two rings on each side with your fingers, stretch it out to about 1 in. in length.

2. Cut a 6–8-in. length of black wire. Find the center and bend the wire around one of the shafts of your round-nose pliers. At the point where the wire meets around the shaft of the pliers, pinch the wire with the tips of your flat-nose pliers to form a loop, with both ends of the wire running parallel to each other.

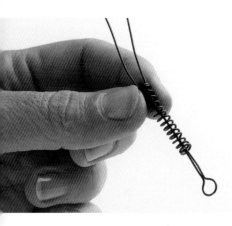

3. Thread this wire through the stretched coil, pulling it right up to the loop.

4. Thread one green seed bead onto each extended wire. Using your round-nose pliers, form an open spiral at the end of each wire to create the butterfly's antennae. Gently hammer the spirals on a steel block to work harden them (see page 21).

5. Cut a piece of black wire 1 in. longer than the butterfly. Thread on a 5mm green wood bead and form a head pin at one end (see page 14). Push the wire through the coil, as shown.

6. Using your round-nose pliers, form a link at the other end of the wire (see page 13).

7. Cut a 6-in. length of black wire. Place the center of the wire about three-quarters of the way up the coil, and wrap it around once or twice, leaving about 1½ in. of wire extending on either side. Thread each extending wire with about 30 black and green seed beads, leaving about ½ in. of wire extending on each side.

8. Using your round-nose pliers, form a small, tight spiral at each end of the protruding wires. Using your fingers, curl the beaded wires around in concentric circles to form a "wing" on each side of the central coil.

9. Decide how long you want your necklace to be and cut two pieces of cord in each color to this length. Bind all the cords together at one end with a small piece of masking tape. Secure the bound end in a vise, and braid (see page 17). Secure the other end with another piece of masking tape.

10. Using your round-nose pliers, make a coiled fish-hook clasp and fastener from 24-gauge black wire (see page 20). Slip the "eye" of the fastener onto one end of the cord, and squeeze the last loop of the coil with your flat-nose pliers to secure. If you wish, put a tiny dab of Superglue onto the end of the cord for added security.

ABOVE

Make a jacket lapel or hat pin by threading a ready-made lapel-pin finding through the central coil. These butterflies would also look very decorative placed in your potted plants!

11. Slip the butterfly motif onto the cord. Slip the fish-hook clasp onto the other end of the cord, and secure in the same way as the eye.

chapter 5
accessories

I hope the projects in this chapter will inspire you to consider designing and fabricating matching accessories and wire art to complement your own jewelry pieces. Jewelry is highly personal and these projects, which include a key ring, handbag clip, and hair grip, provide great gift ideas for special birthdays and anniversaries.

charm cascade clip

Cascading down like bubbles in a waterfall, the beads are encased in spirals of wire to form a unified bunch that can be used to decorate a key ring, handbag, or belt clip, or suspended from a cord as a necklace. Match the color of the beads and cord to the color of your bag or belt. I used relatively small beads, to keep the design light and delicate. To encase larger beads, simply increase the amount of wire that you use.

OPPOSITE

Clip the charm cascade onto a belt, a handbag, or even a cellphone cover as a colorful and trendy fashion accessory. You can make the "cascade" as light or as full as you wish.

You will need

10 x 6–8 mm round hematite (or black) beads

6 x 0.4mm silver round beads

20-gauge silver wire

Black cotton cord

Ready-made key-ring clip

Round- and flat-nose pliers

Wire cutters

Superglue (optional)

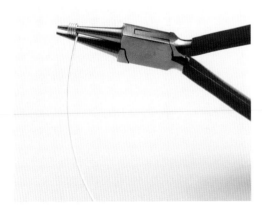

1. Cut a 12–14-in. length of black cotton cord. Using the tips of your round-nose pliers, shape 20-gauge silver wire into a coil, just as you would when making jump rings (see page 16). Feed the end of the cord into the coil, making sure that the cord will fit inside the coil when doubled.

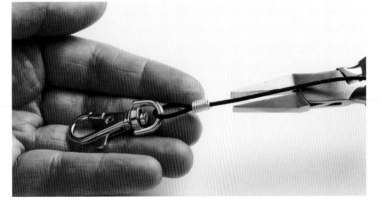

2. Fold the cord about 2 in. from the end to form a loop. Thread the end of the cord through the link of the ready-made key-ring clip and back through the coil of wire. Using the tips of your flat-nose pliers, squeeze the last ring of the coil on each side to secure the coil on the cord. (If you wish, you can put a tiny dab of superglue inside the coil for extra support.)

3. Cut about 6 in. of 20-gauge silver wire. Find the center of the wire, and twist it around the tips of your round-nose pliers to form a little circle.

4. Holding the wire tightly in your flat-nose pliers, curl one end to create an open spiral approximately the same size as the beads that you are going to encase. Spiral the other end of the wire in the same way, making sure that each side curls in the opposite direction, like the letter "S."

5. Place a bead firmly against one of the spirals, and fold the opposite spiral over it to encase it.

6. Using your flat-nose pliers, pull the central loop of the spiral upright to make a suspension link, and spend a little time making sure that the wire sits tightly and evenly around the bead. Use your fingers to mold the wire around each bead so that it is snugly encased.

7. Once you have encased all the beads, make six tight spirals threaded at the top with 0.4mm silver beads. Make 16 jump rings (see page 16).

8. Connect each spiral and encased bead to a jump ring. Suspend the spirals and beads from the cord, placing a couple of silver spirals at the top, middle, and base, and tying and knotting the cord around each jump ring. When all the encased beads and spirals have been threaded onto the cord, tie a final knot at the end of the cord.

ABOVE

This design could also be used as a key ring (top), or constructed with more cord to make a necklace, bracelet, or anklet (bottom).

salmon key ring

BELOW
This key ring makes an ideal gift—and it's ever so quick to make! Try making it with different colors of beads and wire for different sets of door or car keys.

This easy-to-make key ring incorporates a simple fish shape filled in with beads in pink, salmony colors. The Celts commonly used stylized animal patterns, known as zoomorphs, in their designs, believing that they would thus miraculously be endowed with the animal's characteristics, and the salmon was associated with knowledge. According to Irish Celtic mythology, a salmon ate the nine acorns that fell from the Tree of Knowledge into the River Boyne and gained all the knowledge in the world. A druid foretold that the first person to eat of its flesh would gain its magical powers and have knowledge of all things— and that person was none other than the legendary Celtic hero, Fionn mac Cumhail (Finn McCool).

You will need

20-gauge copper wire

28-gauge copper wire

Size 11 seed beads in pink/salmon colors

2mm glass crystals

1 x 4 mm copper bead

Key-ring finding

Round- and flat-nose pliers

Wire cutters

Hammer and steel stake

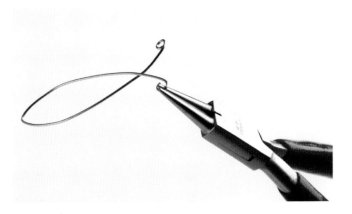

1. To make a salmon fish frame about 1¾ in. long, cut about 5 in. of 20-gauge copper wire. Using the tips of your round-nose pliers, find the center of the wire and bend each side up until the wires cross over, about 2 in. from the end. Using the tips of your round-nose pliers, curl a small loop at the end of each wire.

2. Holding the loop firmly in your flat-nose pliers, form an open spiral on each side curling outward, away from each other. Gently hammer the end of the spirals on a steel stake, avoiding the crossed-over wires.

3. Cut approximately 10 in. of 28-gauge copper wire, and wrap it several times around the crossed-over wires at the base of the spirals. Begin threading this fine wire with small seed beads, wrapping the wire around the top and bottom of the frame to fill the void.

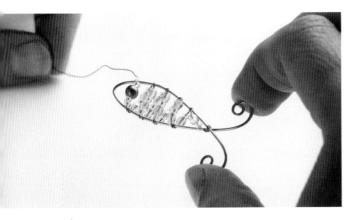

4. As you approach the "head" of the fish, thread the 4mm copper bead onto the wire to make the "eye" and secure the end of the wire around the frame. Cut off any excess wire and neaten the end (see page 17).

5. Make a jump ring from 20-gauge copper wire (see page 16), and suspend the salmon motif from a ready-made key-ring finding.

pictish cufflinks

You will need

20-gauge copper wire

2 flat-topped bone- or shell-effect buttons, ¾ in. in diameter

4 x size 8 seed black beads

Round- and flat-nose pliers

Wire cutters

Hammer and steel stake

Superglue

The Picts were a confederation of tribes that came together to oppose the Roman occupation of Britain and then occupied the central and eastern parts of Scotland for several hundred years after the Romans' departure. They left a legacy of intricate stone carvings, which date back to around 650–850 CE. These large, cross-shaped slabs have stories depicted in panels, embellished with spirals and interlaced knotwork patterns. This cufflink design was taken from a fragment of one such carving.

1. Cut two 2-in. lengths of 20-gauge copper wire. Using your round-nose pliers, curl each one into small open spiral, slightly smaller in diameter than your chosen buttons (see page 15). Gently "stroke" hammer each spiral on a steel stake to flatten and work-harden it (see page 21). Glue one spiral onto the top of each button.

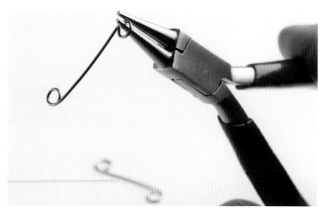

2. Cut two 2-in. lengths of 20-gauge copper wire and form a small circle at one end by wrapping the wire around the fattest part of your round-nose pliers. Turn the wire over and form another circle at the other end, curling it in the opposite direction to form an elongated figure eight.

3. Continue curling the circles in toward each other, until they meet in the center. Gently "stroke" hammer each unit on a steel stake to flatten and work-harden it (see page 21).

4. To form the bars of the cufflinks, cut two 2-in. lengths of 20-gauge copper wire. Find the center of each wire and, using the tips of your round-nose pliers, twist the wire around until it crosses over itself, forming a small circle in the center of each piece.

ABOVE
Buttons topped with a wire swirl make attractive cufflinks. You must use buttons with a shank, so you can attach the cufflink bar.

5. Using 20-gauge copper wire, make four small coils about ¼ in. long, just as you would when making jump rings (see page 16). Thread one seed bead up to the small central circle of wire on the bar, then add a coil of wire. Repeat on the other side of the bar, and form a tight spiral at each end (see page 15). Twist the spirals through 90°, and push them flat against the wire coils to fill the ends of the coils. Repeat for the second cufflink.

6. Make two large jump rings from 20-gauge copper wire (see page 16). Thread one jump ring through the shank of each button. Make two more jump rings to link the figure eight units to the beaded bars of the cufflinks. Connect one bar to the link on the back of each button.

shamrock
hair grip

You will need

20-gauge green wire

Barrette hair grip

4 in. brown suede cord

Masking tape

Round- and flat-nose pliers

Wire cutters

According to legend, the shamrock, with its three leaves, was used by St Patrick to demonstrate the Holy Trinity when converting the Celts to Christianity. It has since been adopted as the national emblem of Ireland. Created from three wire "heart" shapes, this design can also be threaded with beads and used as the center of a hair band, or as a tiara for a bridesmaid's head dress.

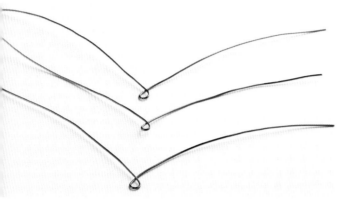

1. Cut three 9-in. lengths of 20-gauge green wire. Place your round-nose pliers just past the center of each piece, and curl the wire around the pliers until it crosses over.

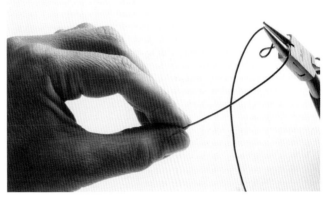

2. Place the fattest part of your round-nose pliers on one side of the loop that you have just created, and pull the wire down. Repeat on the other side, crossing the ends over to form a "heart" shape.

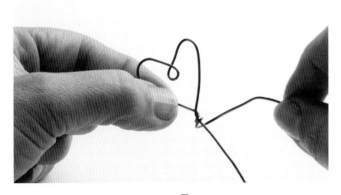

3. Twist and wrap the shorter end of wire around the other stem to secure the base of the heart. Cut off any excess and neaten the end (see page 17).

OPPOSITE

Make the same design using different colored wires, or thread beads onto the wire for a chunkier hair grip. Alternatively, use pearls and crystal beads and wire the shamrock onto a tiara base to make a bridesmaid's headdress.

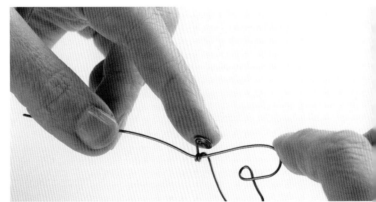

4. Using your round-nose pliers, form a small, tight spiral at the end of the wire (see page 15). Press it down with your fingers to hide the wrapped wire stem.

5. Wrap 20-gauge green wire around the shaft of your round-nose pliers, just as you would when making jump rings (see page 16), to form a coil about ¼ in. long. Cut the coil off the spool of wire, leaving about 1 in. projecting.

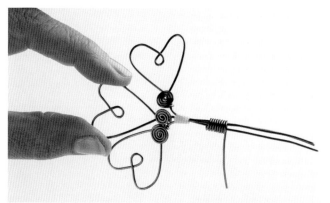

6. Using a tiny strip of masking tape, tape the stems of all three hearts together in a bunch just under the spirals, making sure that each spiral faces in the same direction. Thread the taped stems through the center of the coil. Pull two of the heart shapes out to the side to form the "shamrock" shape.

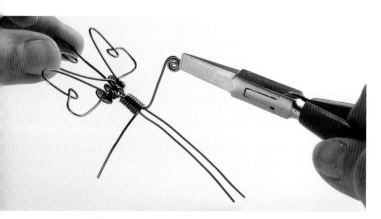

7. Using your round-nose pliers, form a small, tight spiral (see page 15) at the end of the central shamrock stem. Flatten it against the back of the coil to secure. Squeeze the first ring of the coil with your flat-nose pliers to secure it just below the spirals of the shamrock leaves.

8. Form the wire projecting from the end of the coil into a small, tight spiral and the other two shamrock stems into open spirals.

OPPOSITE
Green is the obvious color to choose for this shamrock design, but you could make the hair grip using twisted colored wires for a more vibrant effect.

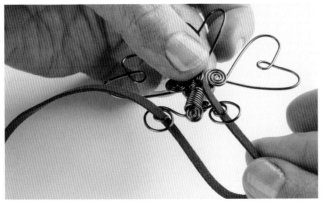

9. Thread the suede cord through the center of one of the open spirals, and then around the back of the coil and up through the center of the other open spiral.

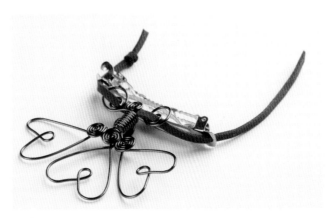

10. Thread the suede cord up through one hole on the barrette hair grip and down through the other. Pull taut and knot on the reverse, as close to the holes as possible.

It is hard to stray from spiral patterns when designing with wire, as it lends itself so readily to being curled and formed in flowing lines. Throughout Celtic art, unbroken lines and spiral patterns were used to symbolize the process of man's eternal spiritual growth. In this bracelet, the spirals are created from double wire, to ensure that the watch strap is not only attractive, but practical and functional for everyday wear.

watch-strap bracelet

OPPOSITE

This classic spiraled wire bracelet makes an original and eye-catching watch strap. It can also be made with colored beads to make it fun and jazzy!

You will need

20-gauge silver wire

18 x size 8 black seed beads

Watch face

Round- and flat-nose pliers

Wire cutters

1. Cut eight 9-in. lengths of 20-gauge silver wire. Using the tips of your round-nose pliers, bend the wire about 2 in. from the end. Thread two black seed beads onto the unbent end, and then bend this end, as shown.

2. Using your flat-nose pliers, squeeze the doubled wires together.

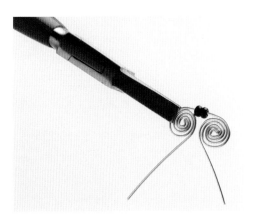

3. Using the tips of your round-nose pliers, curl the very ends of the doubled-up wires into a circle, trying to keep the wires parallel to each other. Continue forming an open spiral on each side, curling them in toward each other so that they meet in the center. Leave just over ½ in. of wire uncurled at each end, to form the links.

4. Pull the ends of the wire around the outside of the spirals so that they protrude on each side. If the wires are too long, cut off any surplus with your wire cutters; they should just extend past the top of the spirals. Form these extending wires into small links (see page 13).

5. Holding each link in turn with your flat-nose pliers, carefully twist them through 90° so that they face each other.

6. Open up the links at the top of each unit, and hook them over the bar of the next unit, so that the beads are in between. Close the links with your flat-nose pliers. Connect four units together for each side of the bracelet.

7. Make two large jump rings (see page 16). Thread one black seed bead onto each one, then thread the jump ring through the top links of the last doubled-spiral unit on each side of the strap, trapping the bead in between.

8. To make the hook of the fastener, cut a 4-in. length of 20-gauge silver wire. Fold it in half, and squeeze the doubled wire together with your flat-nose pliers. Curl the doubled wire around the shaft of your round-nose pliers to form a hook, and then curl the very end up into a little "lip."

9. Twist the stem of doubled wire, just under the hook, and separate the two ends of wire. Using the tips of your round-nose pliers, form a link at the end of each wire (see page 13). Using your flat-nose pliers, twist the links through 90° so that they are at right angles to the hook.

BELOW
The eye of the clasp needs to be at right angles to the hook in order for the bracelet to sit flat on your wrist when it is worn.

10. To make the eye of the fastener, cut a 3-in. length of 20-gauge silver wire. Wrap the center of the wire around the fattest part of your round-nose pliers to form a circle, and twist the wire just underneath. Separate the wires underneath the twist and, using your round-nose pliers, form a link at the end of each wire (see page 13). Attach the hook to the last unit of one section of chain, and the eye to the last unit of the other section, with two seed beads between the links.

jig patterns

The patterns shown here are based on a jig in which the holes are arranged in horizontal rows. If your jig has holes arranged on the diagonal, simply rotate it until the holes are aligned as shown below. For more information on using a jig, turn to page 12.

Shawl stick pin (page 34)

Curl the wire around the pegs as shown, following the direction of the arrows and returning to the center peg between 1 and 2, 3 and 4, 5 and 6, and 7 and 8.

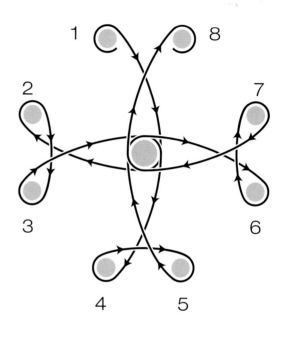

Lindisfarne Choker (page 80)

Curl the wire around the pegs as shown, following the direction of the arrows.

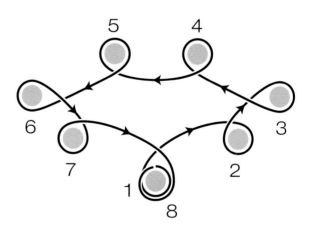

Book of Kells Choker (page 82)

Curl the wire around the pegs as shown, following the arrows and returning to the center peg between 2 and 3, and 5 and 6.

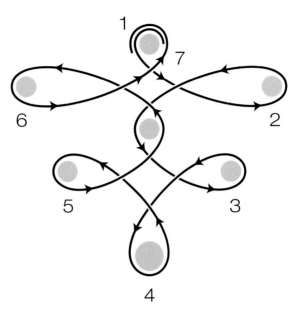

Celtic Cross (page 98)

Curl the wire around the pegs as shown, following the direction of the arrows.

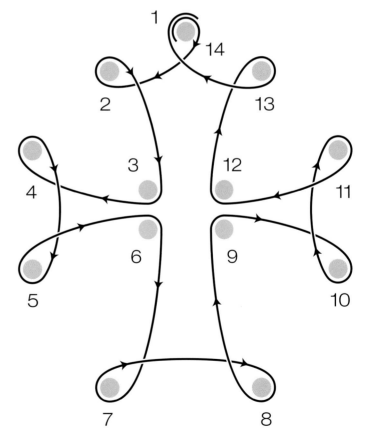

suppliers

U.K. SUPPLIERS

Bead Addict
8 Charter Close
Sale, Cheshire M33 5YG
Tel: 0161 973 1945
www.beadaddict.co.uk

The Bead Shop
21A Tower Street
London WC2H 9NS
Tel: 020 7240 0931
www.beadworks.co.uk

Burhouse Ltd
Quarmby Mill
Tanyard Road
Oakes
Huddersfield
West Yorkshire HD3 4YP
Tel: 01484 655 675
www.burhouse.com

Constellation Beads
The Coach House
Barningham
Richmond
North Yorkshire DL11 7DW
Tel: 01833 621094
www.constellationbeads.co.uk
(On-line sales only)

Cookson Precious Metals
59–83 Vittoria Street
Birmingham B1 3NZ
Tel: 0121 212 6421
www.CooksonGold.com
(Suppliers of steel stakes,
hammers, pliers, sterling
silver and gold wires)

Creative Beadcraft Ltd
20 Beak Street
London W1F 9RE
Tel: 020 7629 9964
www.creativebeadcraft.co.uk

International Craft
Unit 4
The Empire Centre
Imperial Way
Watford WD24 4YH
Tel: 01923 235 336
www.internationalcraft.com

Jilly Beads Ltd
29 Hexham Road
Morecambe
Lancashire LA4 6PE
Tel: 01524 412 727
www.jillybeads.com

**The Rocking Rabbit
Trading Co.**
7 The Green
Haddenham
CB6 3TA
Tel: 0870 606 1588
www.rockingrabbit.co.uk
(On-line and mail-order sales
only)

The Scientific Wire Co.
18 Raven Road
London E18 1HW
Tel: 020 8505 0002
www.wires.co.uk
(Wires only)

Wirejewellery.co.uk
Faulkners Oast (East)
Tonbridge Road
Hadlow
Kent TN11 0AJ
Tel: 01732 850 727
www.wirejewellery.co.uk
(Workshops and starter kits
only)

U.S. SUPPLIERS

CGM Inc.
19611 Ventura Boulevard
Suite 211
Tarzana
CA 91356
Tel: (800) 426 5246
www.cgmfindings.com

Fire Mountain Gems
One Fire Mountain Way
Grants Pass
OR 97526-2373
Tel: (800) 355 2137

Jewelry Supply
Roseville
CA 95678
Tel: (916) 780 9610
www.jewelrysupply.com

Land of Odds
718 Thompson Lane
Ste 123
Nashville
TN 37204
Tel: (615) 292 0610
www.landofodds.com

Mode International Inc.
5111 4th Avenue
Brooklyn, NY 11220
Tel: (800) 663 3527
www.modebeads.com

Rings & Things
P.O. Box 450
Dept. 67-L5
Spokane
WA 99210
Tel: (800) 366 2156
www.rings-things.com

Rio Grande
7500 Bluewater Road. NW
Albuquerque
NM 87121
Tel: (800) 545 6566
www.riogrande.com

Shipwreck Beads
8560 Commerce Place
Dr. NE
Lacey
WA 98516
Tel: (800) 950 4232
www.shipwreckbeads.com

Stormcloud Trading Co.
725 Snelling Ave. N
St. Paul
MN 55104
Tel: (651) 645 0343
www.beadstorm.com

**Thunderbird Supply
Company**
1907 W Historic Rte. 66
Gallup
NM 87301
Tel: (800) 545 7968
www.thunderbirdsupply.com

Wig Jig
P. O. Box 5124
Gaithersburg
MD 20882
www.wigjig.com

www.americanbeads.com
(Online sales only)

index

acknowledgments

There are so many people to thank who have helped make this book possible, but I would never have attempted the Celtic theme if it hadn't been for Cindy Richards (my publisher), who had faith in my abilities and was a great encouragement. Also, mammoth thanks to Sarah Hoggett, my editor, who tirelessly organized, guided, and made inspired suggestions towards the text. To Caroline Arber, whose photography has brought the pieces to life, to Vicky Ling, her assistant, who never complained when asked to model the shamrock hairgrip, to Julie Hailley for her subtle styling, to Sally Powell for her efficiency, and to David Fordham for the book design. In fact, a very big "thank you" to everyone who worked on the book, enabling it to be finally printed and published!